Secrets of the
$uper RICH

DR MICHAEL GILDING

HarperCollins*Publishers*

HarperCollins*Publishers*

First published in Australia in 2002
by HarperCollins*Publishers* Pty Limited
A member of the HarperCollins*Publishers* (Australia) Pty Limited Group
www.harpercollins.com.au

Copyright © Dr Michael Gilding 2002

The right of Dr Michael Gilding to be identified as the moral rights author of this work has been asserted by him in accordance with the
Copyright Amendment (Moral Rights) Act 2000 (Cth).

This book is copyright.
Apart from any fair dealing for the purposes of private study, research, criticism or review, as permitted under the Copyright Act, no part may be reproduced by any process without written permission.
Inquiries should be addressed to the publishers.

HarperCollins*Publishers*
25 Ryde Road, Pymble, Sydney NSW 2073, Australia
31 View Road, Glenfield, Auckland 10, New Zealand
77–85 Fulham Palace Road, London W6 8JB, United Kingdom
Hazelton Lanes, 55 Avenue Road, Suite 2900, Toronto, Ontario, M5R 3L2
and 1995 Markham Road, Scarborough, Ontario, M1B 5M8, Canada
10 East 53rd Street, New York NY 10022, USA

National Library of Australia Cataloguing-in-publication data:

Gilding, Michael.
  Secrets of the Super Rich.
  ISBN 978 0 7322 7386 6.
  1. Rich people–Australia 2. Wealth–Australia I. Title

305.52340994

Cover and internal design by Rose Draper, HarperCollins Design Studio
Typeset by HarperCollins in Optima 10/17

Contents

Acknowledgments vi

1 Meeting the super rich 1

2 Self-made 19

3 A better life 43

4 Driven 65

5 Dynasty 87

6 Inheritance 111

7 Old families 133

8 The big picture 157

References 179

Acknowledgments

I am grateful to many people for their help as I wrote this book. Above all, I am indebted to the individuals who agreed to be interviewed in the first place. They were overwhelmingly generous with their time, their stories and their observations about wealth and society. I am especially appreciative of those individuals who agreed to forego confidentiality (sometimes reluctantly), allowing me to tell stories that I would otherwise have been unable to tell.

My colleagues and students in the School of Social and Behavioural Sciences at Swinburne University of Technology provided a supportive and stimulating environment from the time when I started the project through to its end. Essie Marendy was an excellent research assistant, especially in her work with the interview transcripts. Matilda Langley and Monica Butling provided additional assistance with research and transcription of interviews. The Australian Research Council made the whole project possible, enabling me to fly around Australia to interview individuals from the Rich Lists.

The team at HarperCollins helped me turn the manuscript into a book with consummate professionalism. Thanks especially to Helen Littleton for her keen commitment to the project; Jo Mackay for her skilful coordination of the various tasks; and Devon Mills for his thorough and thoughtful copyediting.

Acknowledgments

Finally, I would not have written this book without the encouragement and support of my wife Sallee McLaren. Sallee encouraged me to interview the super rich in the first place: otherwise I think I would have adopted a much safer type of research strategy that did not involve putting myself on the line in the same way. She also encouraged me to write a book for a wider audience than the usual academic audience. It has not been easy, but it has certainly been rewarding.

This book is dedicated, with love, to Sal.

Dr Michael Gilding
Centre for New Technologies and Society
Swinburne University of Technology, Melbourne
February 2002

The author and publishers gratefully acknowledge permission from the following copyright holders to reproduce the following copyright material.

Business Review Weekly 'Rich 200', Sydney, 16 August 1985, p. 69.

Cadzow, Jane, 'Last of the True Blue Bloods', *The Good Weekend* (magazine within the *Sydney Morning Herald* and *The Age*), 17 November 1990, pp. 10, 18.

Carlyon, Les, *Business Review Weekly* 'Rich 200', Sydney, 14 August 1987, p. 57.

Edgar, Patricia, *Janet Holmes à Court*, HarperCollins, Sydney, 1999, p. 5.

Fairfax, James, *My Regards to Broadway*, Angus&Robertson, Sydney, 1991, pp. 299, 307.

Gottliebsen, Robert, *Business Review Weekly* 'Rich 200', Sydney, 12–18 November 1983.

James, Bill, *Top Deck Daze: Adventures on the Frog and Toad*, Halbrooks Publishing, Avalon, 1999, pp. 15–17.

Krugman, Paul, *The Return of Depression Economics*, Allen Lane, London, 1999, p. 15.

Margo, Jill, *Frank Lowy: pushing the limits*, HarperCollins, Sydney, 2000, pp. 26–7, 55, 66, 89, 185–6, 288.

Myer, Rod, *Living the Dream: the Story of Victor Smorgon*, New Holland Publishers, Sydney, 2000, pp. 285–7.

Ostrow, Ruth, *The New Boy Network: Taking Over Corporate Australia*, William Heinemann, Richmond, 1987, pp. 2, 59, 276.

Power, Phyllis, *From these descended*, Homestead Books, Kilmore, 1997, pp. 167, 174, 178-9.

Uren, David, *Business Review Weekly* 'Rich 200', Sydney, 15 August 1986, p. 47.

Williamson, Kristin, 'Children of the Rich: Living with a sense of entitlement', *The National Times*, 25–31 March 1983, p. 9.

Chapter One

Meeting the super rich

Secrets of the super rich

> 'IT'S FUCKIN' MY MONEY, I'VE EARNED IT, AND THEY CAN KISS MY ARSE.'

I am walking up the stairs. The building is a squat brick block of offices in the suburbs. The stairs are functional concrete. This is not what I'd had in mind when I first imagined interviewing the super rich.

Today's meeting has been difficult to organise. I first wrote to the man several months ago. Later I contacted his office, where I spoke with a very helpful secretary. After several phone calls she told me that the interview was on, but it was then hard to arrange an actual time. I was just about to give up, when it came good.

I wait in the reception area, and then the man I want to interview comes over. He is wearing jeans and an open-necked casual shirt. I feel overdressed in my tie and suit jacket. This is not the first time I have felt overdressed during these interviews.

We make our way to an empty room. It's some type of meeting room — tables and chairs in a rather jumbled order, with a sink, fridge and coffee machine in the corner. He offers me coffee. 'What do you want?' he asks. 'Cappuccino, flat white . . .'

I say I'll have whatever he's having.

'It's going to cost $2.50 whatever you have, so you might as fuckin' well have what you want.'

I think he's joking but I'm not sure. I laugh nervously and say that I'll have a cappuccino.

He begins making the coffee. I ask him whether I can record the interview and he says it's okay. I ask whether he received the list of questions that I faxed through. That's my regular procedure — so that people get a chance to check out the things I'm going to ask them.

He shakes his head. 'I don't read anything, Michael,' he says. 'I don't bother with reading. You see, I don't need to fuckin' read. I don't even use a computer.'

He serves the coffee and we begin the interview. I ask some questions about the annual Rich Lists, published in the *Business Review Weekly*. I ask these questions first because I want to clear the air. The Rich Lists are the reason I have made contact in the first place. More to the point, I have found that people usually want to say something about the Rich Lists — like how much they annoy them. This man is no exception. 'I think they're appalling,' he says.

We speak briefly about the lists, then I ask him about his upbringing. He describes how his father died when he was young and how his mother raised a family 'just by house cleaning and things like that'. 'I had a wonderful upbringing really,' he goes on, 'because we never had anything, which I think is my best asset. My best asset of all, by far, is not being educated. I think that is the big thing wrong with the world today. That's why it is very easy to make money.'

The question of education has come up before in my interviews. I am not rich like the people interviewed, but in most cases I have had more education. Sometimes this gives an edge to the conversation — more so today than any other time, at one point especially.

'You always find that the educated bloke will go the easy way — never goes the hard way — because he's trained that way,' the man reflects. 'As I say, that's why there are only two hard words in any language. What are they? You're an educated man. What are the two hardest words in any language? You don't know!'

I have no idea what he is talking about. All I know is that I'm going to fail the test. 'I've no idea,' I reply.

'See, it's amazing, isn't it,' he declares triumphantly. 'Yes or no!'

For a moment I am still confused; then I understand what he is saying. The two hardest words are yes and no. Educated people never put their heads on the line; they always want to qualify what they say. They never say 'yes' or 'no'. They never take a risk.

'Ah, right, yeah,' I mumble, proving his point.

'Did you sleep with her last night?' he asks.

I'm confused again. What is he going on about now?, I think to myself. 'Sorry?' I say politely.

'Did you sleep with her last night — yes or no?' the man replies emphatically, pleased by my confusion. Then he gets to the point by changing tack. 'Did you get your profit — yes or no? As soon as you get educated people, they never ever take that hard bit. Weak, because they're trained that way. They've got to look at it. They'll say, "Fuck. Oh look, hang on. Oh yes, ah, um" — you know. Fuckin' never yes or no! But when you boil it down, 99 per cent of business is so simple.'

The interview moves on — from childhood to business career, to succession plans, to social issues. At one point I ask about the influence of the old school tie.

'I used to buy Rolls-Royces,' he recalls. 'I bought seven in nine years. I fuckin' went down there one day and I wasn't real well dressed. I'm sure they didn't fuckin' know me. The bloke who usually knows me wasn't there, and they wouldn't fuckin' serve me. So I walked straight across the road and bought a new Ferrari. Fuck them! I'm never going to buy another Rolls-Royce again.

'So, all that you say about the old school tie and the bullshit stuff — yes! I mean, I've never had to worry about it, realistically, because it comes down to simple things — it's fuckin' my money, I've earned it, and they can kiss my arse. Simple as that.'

Simple as that. At the end of the interview I thank him, genuinely. It has been a fascinating interview.

'Well, if it has helped you, Michael, I'm delighted. If it hasn't, it doesn't worry me, you know.'

Then, as we say goodbye, he remarks, 'I enjoyed that', and his voice reveals a mixture of satisfaction and surprise.

Between November 1998 and September 2000 I conduct 50 interviews with individuals drawn from the *Business Review Weekly* Rich Lists. The people I interview — or in some cases the families of the people I interview — are worth at least $60 million. In most cases they are worth a great deal more. The interviews are part of a study on super-wealth in Australia. The magazine *Business Review Weekly* has been publishing its Rich Lists since 1983. I am trying to find out something about the individuals and families identified in the lists. Who are they? How did they become so wealthy? What do they plan to do with their fortunes? How does wealth influence their relationships with other people and society as a whole?

'I ENJOY BEING ON THE *BRW* RICH LISTS AS MUCH AS I'D ENJOY HAVING MY HEAD PUSHED DOWN THE TOILET!'

Secrets of the super rich

For a long time I put off doing the interviews. I cannot imagine anyone on the Rich Lists agreeing to talk with me. I read academic studies of wealth. None of them involve interviews. One American researcher writes that he tried but gave up — partly because no one would talk with him, and partly because the few people who did talk were so guarded about what they said that it wasn't worth the effort.

More to the point, the thought of asking people for interviews makes me anxious. It scares me. At the time, I explain my anxiety in terms of doing 'down-up research'. Most researchers do 'up-down research'. That is, they are up the social ladder, looking down. They study groups that are less powerful than themselves and easily accessible. Individuals in these groups find it difficult to say no. This is why we know more about first year university students than any other social group in the world. They are a captive population.

Researchers tend not to study social groups more powerful than themselves. They are even less inclined to *interview* those more powerful than themselves. People further up the social ladder find it easier to say no. They are also confident in challenging the researcher. It is a much tougher research assignment. And it doesn't get much more difficult than interviewing the super rich.

This seems a very plausible reason for my anxiety. I later realise, though, that there is more to it than this. I am anxious because I want to ask questions about personal money. A book by the Australian political scientist Valerie Wilson, entitled *The Secret Life of Money*, draws my attention to a general taboo across income groups in relation to talking about personal money. As Wilson observes, personal money is associated with achievement, prestige, power, failure and humiliation. It arouses the full gamut of emotions, including fascination, curiosity, envy, prudishness and embarrassment. Only food and sex come close in terms of arousing such strong and diverse sentiments. In turn, people are both secretive and sensitive about personal money. They are secretive even with their own immediate family — that is, their parents and their children — quite apart from people outside the family. 'Rich' and 'poor' are taboo words across income groups. No wonder, then, that I feel discomfort in approaching rich people for information about their fortunes. I am breaking a social taboo.

Notwithstanding this, I write letters to ten individuals on the Rich Lists. I explain my research and set out a series of protocols or 'rules' for the project. 'The interview could be anonymous or otherwise,' I tell them, 'depending upon your views and preferences.' I promise to send them the schedule of questions before the actual interview, and a transcript of the interview after completion 'for checking or alteration, as considered appropriate'.

A week passes. I dread making the follow-up phone calls. When the time finally arrives I sit at my desk for an hour with my head in my hands, fearing rejection and embarrassment.

The first phone call is a surprise. I ask for the industrialist in question. I expect to talk with his secretary. Instead, he answers the phone personally, which confuses me. My mouth goes dry. I mumble that I have sent him a letter; he says he has not received it. Stumbling over the words, I say something about doing a study of people on the *Business Review Weekly* Rich Lists. I know that this is not a winning line. I ask for an interview anyway and am amazed when he agrees.

'Give me a ring when you get up here,' he says.

It is scarcely ever so easy again. Altogether I write about 130 letters. In some instances people clearly resent the Rich Lists and any inquiry in relation to their wealth. One man is friendly when I say that I am doing academic research on entrepreneurship, but he changes his tone when I say that my starting point is the Rich Lists.

'I enjoy being on the *BRW* Rich Lists as much as I'd enjoy having my head pushed down the toilet!' he says. He tells me that he will think about my request, but does not return any of my phone calls.

Another man writes in a handwritten letter that the listing 'has caused considerable anguish to the family because of the way it was initially done, the inaccuracy in it, and the editor's refusal to delete it until the family reveals all'. He declines to be interviewed.

Other people are simply unavailable. Often they are overseas. In some instances they are clearly working at a pitch that leaves no time for anything outside business. One personal assistant apologises after several phone calls. 'I don't think it's going to happen, Michael. He's totally preoccupied at the moment. Your timing is probably not right.'

Another man's PA sighs and tries to explain. 'I don't know if you know,' she says, 'but he's 76 years of age and he's still trying to run the company, so he just doesn't get time for this sort of thing.'

Nonetheless, a steady flow of people prove willing to speak with me. Altogether I conduct 16 interviews in Sydney, 16 in Melbourne, 6 in Perth, 5 in Adelaide, 4 in Brisbane, and 3 in other parts of Australia. Of these 50 interviewees, 43 are men and 7 are women. Thirty-four people are entrepreneurs who were largely responsible for accumulating the fortune in the first place. The remaining 16 interviews are with second and third generation family members who hold an ongoing stake in the family fortune. The people agree to talk for a variety of reasons. Often the reasons are interconnected.

First, some people welcome an opportunity to talk about their experiences of wealth with a stranger, whereas they can't readily talk about it with their friends or colleagues — not even with their families. One man says on the phone that he's in the process of working through inheritance issues at the moment. 'These are huge issues you're looking at,' he says. 'Maybe I'll have worked through them by the time I see you.'

He hasn't. He sets aside a large block of time for the interview. He takes the questions very seriously and is thoughtful and open in his replies. For example, he reflects on the process of giving money away. 'What I found is that it's a bit scary when you start, because you've actually worked for this. It's your security. You're giving it away and you can't get it back. If you fall on hard times, nobody is going to give it back to you. So I'm still quite insecure, as crazy as it might sound.'

Second, people are often proud of what they have achieved and see the interview as providing a licence — notwithstanding the taboo on flaunting personal wealth — to talk about their achievements. This is especially the case with self-made men and women. As I approach more people for interviews, I become aware that 'self-made' individuals are most willing to speak with me. One man, for example, reflects that 'most entrepreneurs like myself are "classics" who have started from nothing'. The Rich List, he adds, tickles the ego a bit. 'I could say that the only thing I've achieved in my life is to get on that list. I've got my business and I've got my money, but it's the recognition of me which I pretend I don't like. To be honest, I'd be upset if I weren't on it now.'

In contrast, individuals who inherit big fortunes are the least willing to speak with me.

Third, some people meet me with a broader agenda in mind. They have an axe to grind. For instance, one man sends me an email.

'I wish to point out at the outset that the "Rich List" totally misrepresents our position, and riles us greatly,' he writes. 'Appearing on that list places us under inappropriate expectations from many quarters!

'However, I would be prepared to contribute to your study, in the interests of Family Businesses as a whole, on a confidential basis and under the conditions specified in your letter.'

Another man says that he wants to repair the image of entrepreneurs, damaged in the 1980s. A third says that he thinks it's good for people to understand how wealth is created.

Finally, in some cases people are curious about the project. One man, thinking aloud on the phone, remarks, 'I've often noticed that there are lots of people like me in the States, but hardly any in Australia.'

Another individual reflects on my project at the end of the interview. 'I would be very surprised if you could actually get a common thread through the study that you're undertaking. I would be interested to read your findings at the end.

'I just find that, in my experience, wealth is accumulated through any number of different circumstances ... through any number of different motivations — some inherited, some through personal drive after re-establishing in Australia, after migrating to Australia on ten quid, or what have you.'

> 'OKAY, I TRUST YOU, OTHERWISE I WOULDN'T TALK TO YOU AT ALL. ALRIGHT?'

Many people ask at the end of interviews how others have responded to my questions. The taboo on discussing personal wealth means that they are unsure as to what other people in their position think about these issues. They want to know whether their views are similar or different to the other views I have heard.

In her biography of Janet Holmes à Court, Patricia Edgar describes her first meeting with Robert Holmes à Court. The meeting began inauspiciously when Edgar complimented Holmes à Court on the fuchsias in his office, too nervous to notice that they were artificial. Holmes à Court looked 'long and hard' at the fuchsias, then 'long and hard' at Edgar, and finally said disdainfully, 'I don't do the flowers.'

'Midway through the meeting,' Edgar continues, 'I realised my body was rigid from head to toe and I began to try to release the tension by consciously relaxing my body bit by bit.'

Reading Edgar's account, I experience instant recognition. Edgar was hyper-vigilant, alert to danger. Ironically, her alertness narrowed her focus so that she was less able to respond to her environment. In my first interviews I am also hyper-vigilant, because, like Edgar, I'm entering an unfamiliar environment. Moreover, it's an environment laden with mystique — the mystique of great wealth and power, with echoes from the fairytales and myths of childhood.

For their part, the people I interview are not always sure that they want to be interviewed. They check me out on my arrival, deciding whether to trust me or not. Trust is an issue because the super rich often feel vulnerable. There is enormous prestige associated with great wealth. There is also enormous curiosity, envy and hostility. Moreover, great wealth sometimes generates deep and fractious divisions within families. The people I interview are often suspicious of my motives. They are also worried about what I will do with their stories. It is a long time before I am able to recognise this vulnerability — I feel too vulnerable myself.

Consider, for example, my meeting with Isador Magid, a Melbourne property developer who arrived in Australia as a refugee from Communist China. At the time of the interview, Magid was 84 years of age and still heavily involved in his business. The main thing I knew about him before the interview (from *Business Review Weekly*) was that he was responsible for introducing Twisties to Australia.

Secrets of the super rich

I arrive at Magid's offices, unpack my recording equipment, and ask him whether it is alright to record the interview. He tells me to slow down. 'How can we begin, when I do not know you?' he asks. 'Let us get to know one another first. I must find out first what you are doing and why you are doing it. Then we can decide whether or not we have something to talk about.'

I do my best to explain the project, being mindful of the taboo. I tell him that I am studying entrepreneurship and inheritance. These words are reasonably neutral and non-threatening. I am interested that there are so many new fortunes on the Rich Lists, fortunes often assembled by migrants. I want to understand the 'big picture' of wealth creation in Australia.

Magid looks sceptical. He says — in the nicest possible way — that he does not know the answers to these questions. He does not think that there is anything about his experience that would be helpful. I persist, saying that I am sure he would be able to help me, that his story would be very interesting, especially because he was a migrant. I would like to know how it was possible to build a successful business in Australia despite the disadvantages of being a migrant.

Magid ruminates aloud on some of the issues that I've identified. He starts talking about the perils of family dynasties. I glance at my watch, and then at my cassette recorder. I want to record what he is saying. I ask again whether I can record. He refuses again. He elaborates on the perils of dynasties. We go through this cycle several times. Half an hour later I start to resign myself to the fact that there will be no interview. As I get ready to leave, my disappointment shows. At this point Magid has a change of heart. He explains that he doesn't like to disappoint people who are trying to achieve something for themselves. He agrees to the interview and in the end I see him on three separate occasions, as he conscientiously makes his way through my schedule of questions.

Isador Magid proves unusual — most people proceed directly with the interview. Yet all interviews follow a similar path. They are successful to the extent that I manage to establish rapport, or trust. This involves ongoing negotiation. In one interview, for example, the man breaks off in mid-sentence in an account of a bitter family dispute.

'Where does this go?' he asks abruptly. 'What's happening with this stuff I'm telling you?'

'It's up to you,' I reply.

'I've been very open,' he says.

He has been very open, breathtakingly open. I acknowledge the fact.

'I'm happy to tell you everything,' he says, 'but the fact of the matter is, I don't want my name mentioned. I don't want *anything* to be publicised that's obviously about me, unless you seek my prior approval — and I won't be unreasonable.'

At the end of the interview he stipulates that I must destroy the cassettes and transcripts on completion of the project.

On another occasion the man I'm interviewing pauses to warn me that I can't include what he has just said in my book. It would reveal his identity. He is concerned — like about three-quarters of the interviewees — about remaining anonymous.

'You'll have to take it out of this,' he says. 'Right?'

I have already reassured him concerning confidentiality, but I begin to reassure him again. He interrupts me.

'Just take it out.'

'It'll automatically be taken out,' I affirm.

'Okay,' he says, 'I trust you, otherwise I wouldn't talk to you at all. Alright? Okay? That's fine.'

He trusts me, but only up to a point. When he returns the transcript he has blacked out large passages of conversation that he fears might identify him. He has also blacked out his most controversial opinions — the ones that would have made great quotes for this book.

Trust locks me on the horns of a dilemma. On the one hand, I have to generate trust in order to achieve good interviews. On the other hand, the more I generate trust the more difficult it becomes to use the material.

'I don't want this part in,' says one man. 'This is the part that I don't want recorded! Right? So you've got to give me that bit of respect.'

Another interviewee understands my dilemma well. In the course of the interview he includes some blunt assessments of family members. After I send him the transcript he phones me in a mild panic, worried that he has been indiscreet. At the same time, he emphasises that he does not want to 'spoil' the account for me. 'I'm a marketing man myself,' he says. 'I know you need a good story.'

Every interview is different. One person — quoted at the beginning of this chapter — wears his blue-collar background on his sleeve and swears heavily throughout the interview. Another man, who was a migrant, still struggles with the English language. I find myself smiling a lot in his interview, as we do when language is not enough. One woman I talk with rides to the interview at an inner city café on her scooter. She'd inherited a fortune but takes pains not to be identified by it. Another person with old money has a patrician style. He is very formal, I am very deferential. And so on.

Some interviews struggle to get off the ground, though most do get off. Once they have made an undertaking to speak with me, most people are generous and thoughtful in responding to my questions. The interviews usually last about an hour and a half. A few last much longer.

In the case of Isador Magid, I finally reach the end. 'Look,' I say, 'I've come to the end of all my questions.'

'Good!' Magid says good-humouredly.

'I was going to ask if there was anything that you wanted to add to what you've already said,' I ask conscientiously.

'Ah, you've been very exhausting,' he replies.

He's exhausted, I'm exhausted. I thank him.

'It's a pleasure,' he says graciously.

One interviewee — quoted earlier — questions whether I will be able to find a common thread in my study. He is right to do so. The super rich are a motley crowd. Sometimes I wonder myself whether I will be able to find a common thread.

There are differences in terms of social origin, reflected in the course of the interviews. Some fortunes are passed down from the nineteenth and early twentieth centuries, inherited across generations. Some are assembled by migrants, from every continent around the globe. Some are accumulated by Australian-born entrepreneurs, ranging from individuals with almost no education to those with postgraduate qualifications.

There are also differences in terms of how the fortunes were accumulated. There are media moguls, company raiders and property developers. There are prospectors and movie stars. There are the patriarchs of private empires sitting on a pile of hard assets. There are cyber entrepreneurs, sitting on paper fortunes from public companies that have never turned a profit.

> 'WHY DO YOU WANT TO RUN FASTER? YOU RUN WELL ENOUGH. BUT YOU STILL WANT TO IMPROVE YOURSELF.'

Secrets of the super rich

Not only are there many pathways to wealth. The fortunes vary enormously in their scale. One of the first people I interview is listed near the bottom of the 1998 Rich List, not far from the $60 million point of entry. He says several times during the interview that he is only 'small fry'. Another man comments, 'We've got a few rich families here on the Rich List that you talk about, but that wealth is nothing on international standards, if you take out the Pratts, and Lowy, and Packer and Murdoch.'

'The rest are nothing,' he emphasises. 'When you get down to $500 million, $400 million, $300 million — a lot of that money is at risk. It's not as if it's stabilised wealth.'

At first I am bemused by these protests. Sixty million dollars seems a lot to me. Five hundred million dollars looks perfectly secure. But after a year of interviews I am more sympathetic. The super rich measure wealth with a different yardstick. There are the rich. There are the super rich. There are the super super rich.

Yet there *are* common threads among the interviews, notwithstanding the differences. Here's one example.

I ask Isador Magid what motivated him to grow his business. At first he is reluctant to reply. 'It's too difficult a question to answer,' he says.

'Is it?' I ask.

'Well, listen,' he says. 'It's time now. What makes you spend time talking on such a boring thing? And yet you do it.'

He is referring to my questions about his life and motivation.

'Why do you do it?' he continues. 'You have curiosity. You have an interest in somebody's life which is entirely different from your life. You read so many biographies about different people. You want to know how other people live and how they think.'

Magid returns to his own motivation. He had 'parents and

children to support'. Yet he also had 'that tiny enduring spirit'.

'My business became my obsession,' he says. He pauses, then goes on. 'Why do you do it? It's like a sport. Why do you want to run faster? You run well enough. But you still want to improve yourself.

'Or you have imagination and you think, I can create something, just like a painting. You have nothing and then you start painting, good or bad — well, you'll see later how it works out. People either accept it or they don't accept it, but it's a challenge.'

Magid is more lyrical than most of the people I interview. Nobody else uses the metaphor of art to explain their motivation. Yet overwhelmingly the entrepreneurs I talk with explain their motivation in terms of a challenge. They emphasise that it is not the money, it's the achievement. This is a common thread.

Another common thread emerges when an interviewee describes a delicate game of brinkmanship in the course of an intense family conflict. The family, she observes, has 'this obsessive need for privacy, not to let the neighbours really know what is going on behind closed doors'. She wants to apply enough pressure through the legal process to bring her family to the negotiating table over the distribution of an inheritance.

The woman warns that what she has done so far is only the tip of the iceberg. 'If they want to persevere,' she says, 'I have enough material to fill a book. Would you write it for me?'

I laugh. It is a rhetorical question — I think.

'I have enough material on how a family in business operates behind closed doors in this manner,' she continues. 'They're very private and they really wouldn't want a lot of information to get out. I understand that and I certainly wouldn't do it willingly, but they're playing dirty with me.'

The stakes can be high. There are strong pressures that keep stories such as this one out of sight. The woman's complaint is itself the tip of an iceberg, in that it suggests a larger body of family conflict around the succession of next-generation members to positions of wealth and authority. Other interviews bear this out. So do the occasional family brawls — the Fairfax family in the 1980s, the Moran family in the 1990s, the Belgiorno-Nettis family in the 2000s — that break out into the public sphere, notwithstanding the heavy costs.

The interviews don't tell the whole story, but they have a story to tell. More than this, they allow us to gauge the deeper structures and processes that lie beneath the surface of great personal and family wealth.

Chapter Two

Self-made

> 'SO THIS WAS LIKE THE BIG DREAM: I COULD ACTUALLY GET MONEY AND BUY SOMETHING!'

Andrew Kelly's father died when he was young. His mother ran a milk bar in working-class North Strathfield, in Sydney's inner western suburbs. From a young age Kelly helped out in the milk bar, along with his older brother and sisters. When he was seven he pulled the trolley for his brother on his paper run. 'But I didn't get any money,' he says. At the age of ten he got his own run.

'I was excited about doing a paper run,' Kelly explains, 'because it got me out of working in the shop, where I didn't get paid. I was doing a run and I could earn my own money. When I saved my money, I could buy something with it, you know. So this was like the big dream: I could actually get money and buy something!'

Kelly went to the local state school, but he was more interested in his various entrepreneurial ventures than he was in school. 'Right through to my HSC,' he recalls, 'I went from paper runs to chemist runs, to building bikes in the backyard, to buying cars and pulling them apart.

'I went to buy some bucket seats and they were like $200 and I thought, well, I can buy a whole car for fifty. So I bought another smashed car for fifty, put its bucket seats in my car, sold the rest of the smashed car and got $300.

'I thought, wow, I've just made all that money! So then in that same year I did that about fifteen times — bought all these cars and pulled them apart.'

Following high school Kelly went to the local TAFE college, but he was bored. He wanted a job with some responsibility, and set his sights on being a trainee manager. A succession of interviews went nowhere. A neighbour suggested a 'good job' on the railways. Kelly made his way to the Urban Transit Authority.

'I went there,' he recalls, 'and lined up to fill in the application forms, but the people there said to me, "Oh, you wear glasses. We don't employ people with glasses." I thought, Aah, this is the end!'

The Urban Transport Authority was not only looking for train drivers, but also bus conductors. Kelly got a job as a conductor. The work involved broken shifts, with five hours off in the middle of the day. There was a lot of spare time. One day his uncle showed him some key rings with a tape measure attachment. Kelly bought $50 worth of the key rings and started selling them in his spare time. Then he sold them to shops. In the first four weeks he sold about 5000 of the rings. Then he got a stall at the market and sold them there.

After a few weeks he realised that he was flooding the market and needed new products. He looked up 'Wholesalers' in the Yellow Pages and found some located near his workplace. He started to hang around them every day. 'I was like a kid, and they used to talk to me and educate me,' he recalls. He bought new stock, including car radios. Then he bought a new van so he could carry more stock. Then he employed people to sell the stock. Then he opened a double stand at the market, and a stand at another market. Then he took on more employees. And so on.

In 1980, after eighteen months at the markets, Kelly reassessed his position. He gave up his job on the buses. 'I felt like I was losing blood when I did that,' he says sincerely, 'because I was part of something there.' He'd known lots of people on the buses, and the regular wage provided security.

Kelly now opened a shop — Strathfield Car Radios — at the front of his brother's mechanical workshop. 'It was a decision I made and I didn't make it lightly,' he says. 'But once I had made the decision, I didn't look back and I just had to go for it.'

He expanded from one shop to a chain of shops — some owned by himself, some of them franchises. He painted his shops red, winning publicity and notoriety. He diversified from car radios to mobile phones, keeping one step ahead of the fast-moving youth market, and he built a head office. By the early 1990s the business was energetic but chaotic. 'The bank got a consultant to come in because they thought, if this guy keeps going like this, clocking up millions of dollars of debt — everything written on pieces of paper from when the business was smaller and unprofessional — someone is going to rip him off. But it's just that I was dealing with people I trusted.'

The consultant told him to put in new structures and procedures. Kelly 'kicked him out'. Three months later he introduced the new structures and procedures.

About the same time, lawyers introduced Kelly to the idea of floating his business in the stock market. 'I thought, well, if I can grow these businesses, make some acquisitions, put all the systems in, and consolidate the cost centres, we'd have a profitable business. We'll float to repay the debt and grow, and then everything will be fine.'

Everything did work out fine. The business went from strength to strength and Kelly joined the *BRW* Rich 200 in 1999. His wealth was there on the public record, through his public company.

'My opinion of the lists is that they are pretty accurate,' he says, although he observes that a lot of people want to be totally secretive. In 1999 *BRW* calculated that Kelly was worth $125 million. The fortune ballooned with the stockmarket boom but then contracted to $110 million in 2001, in the wake of the downturn.

Bob Clifford's father came of age in the Depression and found work as a butcher. 'It was a job that he hated all his life,' Clifford says, 'and he always wished that he was doing something else.' Clifford recalls as a child seeing his father try four or five different ventures. In each case, though, he had to go back to his butchering. Nonetheless, he did well enough as a butcher to send his son to Hutchins School, one of Hobart's more exclusive colleges. Clifford enjoyed school and was good at sport, but consistently failed 'classroom things'. He now thinks that he may have suffered from some form of dyslexia. 'I'd look at the problem and I knew the answer, but I didn't quite understand how I got the answer.'

'I THOUGHT, IF THESE POMS CAN BUILD 34 HEAPS OF JUNK LIKE THIS, WE'VE GOT TO BE ABLE TO DO BETTER.'

At fifteen Clifford failed his external examinations. He didn't even try to pass. He knew it was time to leave school, but had no idea what he was going to do. He eventually got an apprenticeship in a backyard printing shop, which he enjoyed. He could not see a future for himself in the business, though. His boss had children coming into it and the set-up costs in the industry were substantial. 'I would have been an employee all my life,' Clifford says. His father now offered a way out, buying several fishing boats on credit and persuading the son to have a go at it. Father and son struggled for five years, because they 'didn't

Secrets of the super rich

really know the business'. Then Clifford decided that they needed a different type of boat.

'We went to a professional builder, and he had an offsider. So the two of them built the boat — technically. But in practice I did all the purchasing, I did a lot of the design work, I did a lot of the organising of it with my father and I did all the labouring.' The boat was a success. 'Went out and caught lots of fish,' he says with satisfaction.

After a few more years, Clifford — now in his late twenties — wanted to do something different. He built and operated a ferryboat on the Derwent River, mostly doing night charters. In 1975 a 10 000 tonne freighter plunged into the Tasman Bridge, destroying the crossing. Clifford's ferries suddenly became an essential part of Hobart's transport system. Clifford seized the opportunity. He met the demand for transport across the river. He built more boats. The business thrived.

He also hired a British hovercraft. 'It was an absolute heap of rubbish, really,' he says. 'It was an absolute nightmare to maintain and, economically, it was by far the least successful boat we had.' Yet this hovercraft had been the 34th on the production line of the British manufacturers. 'But customers loved the idea of going fast and were even prepared to pay double the fare.

'I thought, if these Poms can build 34 heaps of junk like this, we've got to be able to do better. I think that was the first realisation that we didn't need to have excuses for what we were capable of doing — you know, "because we're Tasmanians, we can't do it as well as anyone else". So the typical Tasmanian inferiority complex was washed away.'

The hovercraft experience led Clifford to build a high-speed catamaran. It was fast but ugly. 'Didn't look fast; didn't look right,' he remarks. Then he built an aluminium catamaran, which was an instant success. After another fifteen or so boats (mostly for the Queensland tourist trade), Clifford had flooded the market for passenger boats in

Australia. 'If we were were going to go bigger, we had to go *much* bigger. It had to be, say, a Bass Strait ferry. It had to be able to carry cars.

'But we really didn't have much choice. We either had to stay at a decreasing market share with a work crew of 40, or we had to bite the bullet and go much bigger to a bigger market share.'

In 1999 Clifford's private company finally came to the attention of the *BRW*. 'We're a private company,' Clifford observes. 'I understand that the reason we're on the list is that we're a competitor of a public company, and the public company's figures are well known. We're bigger than they are, and so therefore we should be on the list.' In 2001 *BRW* estimated that the business was worth $180 million.

Nine months later the core companies of the business were in receivership. Clifford insists that the business has seen worse times before, and that he only owed $80 million, with assets of five times this amount.

Imelda Roche was the second of six children. She spent much of her first seven years living with her grandmother. 'My young parents were struggling to manage with three little girls, born a year apart, in a one-bedroom apartment,' Roche explains. 'My grandmother was nursing my father's older sister, who was dying of tuberculosis. I was fortunate enough to be her favourite granddaughter so she offered to take care of me. I think I was as much a companion for my grandmother as she was a carer for me. I still treasure those early years with her.'

At the age of seven Roche returned to live full-time with her parents. The household was always

> 'I MADE A DECISION VERY EARLY IN LIFE THAT, WHATEVER IT TOOK, I WAS GOING TO BECOME FINANCIALLY SELF-RELIANT.'

financially precarious, as her father — a sometime journalist who wanted to be a writer — was often out of work. As a result her mother had to take in whatever work she could find. 'I suppose,' Roche reflects, 'I made a decision very early in life that, whatever it took, I was going to become financially self-reliant.'

Roche went to the local convent school, St Clare's College. When she was fifteen her father — who had started a small suburban newspaper — wanted help in the office. 'So it was decided,' she recalls, 'that I should leave school and help him.' She worked for eighteen months without pay, before striking out on her own. Roche got a job as a bookkeeper and pay clerk at the Imperial Services Club in the City of Sydney and then another four or five jobs in succession.

'Basically I was looking to improve my income-earning capacity,' she says. 'That was the thing that I went after with each change. At the same time I also took on a night job teaching ballroom dancing, and I was working on the weekends as well, looking after children. So my whole focus was on accumulating income and getting some financial security behind me.'

In 1956 she met her future husband. Bill Roche was a sales representative for Kelloggs, the breakfast cereal company. Imelda was now working for another American multinational, National Cash Registers, training checkout operators. When the couple decided to marry, they wanted to make their financial security more certain, and resolved to create another income stream. This was the era when Australian families were buying their first television sets. There was a widespread belief that television caused eye damage unless a lamp was placed on the set.

'We thought, well here's an opportunity; we'll make television lamps. So we set up the manufacturing in my mother's living room and Bill's mother's living room, and coerced all the family members to help wherever they could.'

Bill's brothers sold the lamps on time payment from door to door. When they returned to collect payments, people asked what else they had to sell. So the couple diversified, first into manchester and then into fashion.

'At that stage we had no experience with fashion,' Roche recalls, 'but I thought that it just took some basic common sense combined with a little flair. It was a matter of really looking at what was being promoted in the fashion magazines, in *The Women's Weekly*, and in the *Vogue*, *Simplicity* and *Butterick* pattern books.'

Roche became the designer. The couple arranged for manufacturers to make the clothes. Then they recruited a team of saleswomen to sell the fashions door to door. The business expanded from Sydney to Newcastle and to Melbourne. As it expanded, the couple gave up their day jobs.

By 1968 Roche — now in her mid-thirties — was ready to explore other avenues for direct-selling. She saw an advertisement in the daily tabloid, *The Sun*, seeking management for an American direct-selling company about to begin operations in Australia. Its main product line — which later became the name of the company — was Nutri-Metics, a range of skin care products based on natural ingredients. Roche replied to the advertisement. Three months later the couple had signed on to manage the Australian start-up.

They threw themselves into the new business, working long hours and travelling constantly. The business grew exponentially. At the end of the first year they had recruited 1300 consultants to sell products from their homes. The consultants were mostly women — this was an era when married women were joining the workforce and looking for flexible employment. By the early 1970s the business was manufacturing locally and expanding into the Asia-Pacific region.

Secrets of the super rich

'When we started our first overseas expansion into New Zealand and Singapore,' Roche says, 'I saw that there were no bounds. It would really depend on the amount of commitment and energy and dedication we gave to the business, and our success in sharing our vision with others.'

The Australian arm of the business was by far the most successful. In 1991 the Roches bought out the parent company, finally bringing them to public attention — including the *BRW* researchers. *BRW* valued the couple at $30 million, but then progressively revised its valuations upwards as the scale of the business became more apparent. In 2001 — four years after the Roches had sold the business to the American multinational Sara Lee for a confidential sum — *BRW* estimated that the pair were worth $279 million.

'I think their assumptions are very much hit-and-miss,' Roche comments. 'I dislike intensely being included in such a list. However, it seems to me that, once you are captured, you remain captured, until such time as you may find yourself in a very diminished situation in their eyes.'

'I DIDN'T EVEN KNOW ABOUT THE STOCKMARKET, UNTIL THERE WAS A STOCKMARKET CRASH IN 1987.'

In the early 1960s Ernie Campbell, a full-time Communist Party organiser, produced a book entitled The Sixty Rich Families Who Own Australia. It was the first 'Rich List' in Australia. The list included names that are still well known today — for example the Packers and Fairfaxes in Sydney, and the Baillieus and Myers in Melbourne (but not the Murdochs). These families, Campbell declared, were 'the real owners and rulers of Australia'.

One of Campbell's main points was that rich families are able to transmit their privileges from one generation to the next. There is a long tradition of social science research that makes much the same point. The rich overwhelmingly leave their money to their children. They are also able to give their children a running start in their careers. The rich buy the best education for their children at the top private schools. They provide their children with jobs in the family firm, start-up money for new businesses, and excellent business networks.

The most renowned individuals who have featured in the Rich Lists — Kerry Packer and Rupert Murdoch — are case studies of how big wealth is passed down the generations. Their fathers, Sir Frank Packer and Sir Keith Murdoch, were powerful and wealthy. Both Packer and Murdoch attended Geelong Grammar, the elite school of the era. Kerry Packer inherited a media empire, including the Nine Network and some of the biggest circulation magazines in Australia. Rupert Murdoch's inheritance — an evening tabloid in Adelaide — was modest by comparison, but still large by common standards. Both men have used their inheritance to build much bigger fortunes. Their own sons are now poised to take over their empires.

The Rich Lists have also featured many 'old money' names, whose fortunes were first assembled in the nineteenth century and whose children attended the elite schools across generations. There is the Clarke family in Melbourne. William 'Big' Clarke was the Kerry Packer of the nineteenth century, the richest man in the land. There is the Fairfax family in Sydney, a pillar of the Sydney Establishment by the late nineteenth century. There is the Barr-Smith family in Adelaide, a pillar of the Adelaide Establishment during the same period. Each of these families sent their children to Geelong Grammar. They fit all of the stereotypes of 'big wealth' and social privilege handed down across generations.

Yet Packer and Murdoch are not typical of the people on the Rich Lists. Nor are the Clarkes, Fairfaxes and Barr-Smiths. Above all, they are not typical because their wealth is — by Australian standards — relatively old. Even the Packers and Murdochs date back only to the 1920s and 1930s. But the overwhelming majority of fortunes on the Rich Lists (between 80 and 90 per cent) date back no further than the 1950s.

Consider Ernie Campbell's *The Sixty Rich Families Who Own Australia* — a list of the big Australian fortunes in the middle of the postwar boom. The inaugural *BRW* Rich List in 1983 included only twelve of these sixty fortunes. By 2001 the list was twice the size, but just seven of Campbell's sixty were still on it.

Thanks to their long history a lot of information is readily available about the old fortunes. I didn't need to interview Kerry Packer or Rupert Murdoch in order to establish their fathers' occupations and their school backgrounds. There are biographies of Sir Frank Packer and Kerry Packer. There are at least three biographies of Rupert Murdoch. There are also books and feature articles about the Clarkes, the Fairfaxes and the Barr-Smiths. Anybody can go to a library and discover within half an hour the story of these families.

This is not the case for most of the individuals now on the Rich List. Most of them have more obscure social origins. This is because — like Imelda Roche, Bob Clifford and Andrew Kelly — they did not inherit their fortunes. They are mostly self-made. It is often difficult to find background information about these people. In some cases it is even difficult to work out how and when they made their fortune. The most accessible information on them is school background, at least for those entrepreneurs who attended school in Australia. School background provides a rough measure of social background: there are not many tycoons who send their children to the local government or parish school, and there are not many labourers who send their children to the elite private schools. Generally speaking, children who attend Protestant schools come from more affluent backgrounds than those who attend government and Catholic schools.

Take, for example, the 1998 Rich List. There were 199 entries, of which 177 (89%) were postwar fortunes. Of these, 108 belonged to entrepreneurs who went to school in Australia. (The balance were migrants, who were educated in their country of origin.) I was able to find out the school background of 64 of these entrepreneurs. More than half (52%) attended government schools, like Andrew Kelly. One-quarter (25%) attended elite Protestant schools, like Bob Clifford. One-fifth (20%) — including Imelda Roche — went to Catholic schools, mostly local parish schools. The remaining entrepreneurs (3%) attended Jewish schools.

Even those entrepreneurs who had their start in the elite Protestant system — such as Bob Clifford — often came from relatively modest backgrounds. As I conduct my interviews, I am increasingly impressed not only by the extraordinariness of people's fortunes, but also by the ordinariness of their backgrounds.

Andrew Kelly is especially open about his naivety along the way. 'I didn't even know about the stockmarket,' he says at one point, 'until there was a stockmarket crash in 1987. Someone said the market has crashed. I said, "What market? Business has been really good!" Everything was booming in our retail business.' Kelly floated his business in 1998. One year later he was among Australia's super rich.

The stories of Andrew Kelly, Bob Clifford and Imelda Roche give some idea of the diversity among the super rich — but only some

> 'MONEY WAS THE OBSTACLE, NOT EDUCATION, IN TERMS OF GETTING MY OWN BUSINESS STARTED.'

idea. The diversity is much greater than their stories indicate. At one extreme, the company raider Robert Holmes à Court, who dominated the list in the mid-1980s, came from an aristocratic lineage and attended elite schools in South Africa. At the other extreme, the Channel Seven boss Kerry Stokes was adopted from an orphanage, attended thirteen primary schools as his parents chased work around the country, and could neither spell nor write at the age of fourteen when he ran away from home.

The stories of the super rich may be diverse and idiosyncratic but certain themes run through them. First, the parents of those I talked with overwhelmingly owned their own businesses or were self-employed. They included farmers, shopkeepers, accountants, builders, cabinetmakers and prospectors. Andrew Kelly's mother operated a milk bar. Bill Clifford's father was a butcher. Imelda Roche's father was a self-employed journalist. And so on.

A few of the businesses were reasonably substantial. One man, for example, says that his father was 'a pretty big chemist' — he had seven shops and a factory. In such circumstances, parents were able to send their children to exclusive private schools.

In many instances, parents were not far from the working class. Sometimes they came into business or self-employment through a trade, such as butchery or carpentry. Sometimes they stumbled into self-employment because they could not find employment. The Perth tycoon Stan Perron, for example, describes his father as 'purely a labouring type of person, really', who moved between wages and self-employment depending on the availability of paid work. 'He used to mine a bit of ore with a few of his mates,' Perron says, 'and put a crushing through now and again, but just to get a bare living.

'I used to live in poor circumstances,' he goes on, 'and I always thought that when I grew up I was going to do better than how my father and mother used to live. We used to live in hessian houses with no floors — just matting on the ground or a filter press from the mine for a floor. Never had an ice box or a refrigerator, or anything like that. Just the old Coolgardie safe.'

I ask Perron where he got his ambition to do better than his parents.

'Possibly from my mother,' he replies. 'My mother was very aggressive. Before my time, she had little shops in mining towns. She was always the one who looked after money. She was very good with finances.

'I remember that we had a house in Kalgoorlie that cost £100, I think it was, in those days. Within a few months she bought the block next door and built a house there for another £75.'

In some cases, fathers passed businesses on to their sons, who built them into really big enterprises. For example, Harold Clough, the owner of a big civil engineering business with projects around the world, was studying in the United States when he decided to go into business for himself.

'The hardest step in going into business is the first step,' he reflects. 'I thought, well, there was my father with his business, why don't I go back and join him?'

Clough's father had been a bricklayer, whose office was on the back veranda of the family home. His business had just one employee. 'So when I joined, we doubled our workforce,' Clough says. His father died five years later, whereupon he took over the business, 'and the thing just carried on from there'.

Above all, parents set an example, encouraging their children to think in terms of setting up their own businesses rather than working for wages. Bob Clifford, for instance, observed his father's various entrepreneurial ventures, and left his first trade because he did not want to work for wages for the rest of his life. Similarly, Andrew Kelly, after serving behind the counter of his mother's milk bar, progressed to various youthful entrepreneurial ventures and to setting up his own shop.

A second theme in the stories of interviewees is that education didn't count for much. A good education and academic success routinely lead children into the professions — the law, medicine, academia (as I know too well) and so on. A profession is a means of reaching a better-than-average income and social status but not a huge fortune. Bill James, who completed an economics degree (with a major in accounting) at the University of Sydney and went on to make a fortune through the discount travel retailer Flight Centre, makes precisely this point. An elite education, he comments, is a recipe for not making money, because it leads to a profession. 'Professionals don't make big money, because the clock has to be working, and they themselves are the only ones who can make the money. So even though you've got the clock running, it's locked at a fixed hourly charge-out rate, so you just can't make any real profits.'

In other words, wealth accumulation depends on tapping into other people's labour. Professionals depend too much on their own labour. When they're not working, they're not making money.

The interviewees overwhelmingly attach little importance to the role of education in their business careers. And in fact I don't meet any school prodigies but I interview more than a few school dropouts. It is a supreme irony that Bob Clifford, who designs state-of-the-art high-speed ferries, failed dismally at school. And Andrew Kelly and Imelda Roche both describe themselves as underperformers at school.

Similarly, Brett Blundy, the founder of the music retail chain Sanity, and one of the youngest of the people I interview, describes himself as a failed sixth former. Blundy went from the local technical high school onto a tertiary orientation program at a TAFE college, where he failed again. 'I would have to be pressed hard to say that I did fail,' he admits. 'I don't say that proudly, it just happens to be a fact. I like to justify it — at that time I was more interested in other things. Certainly, even then, I believed that education was irrelevant.'

I ask him about the pathway to a business career.

'I simply went and got a couple of jobs, and then I decided what I needed was money,' Blundy explains. 'Money was the obstacle, not education, in terms of getting my own business started.'

A third theme in the social background of entrepreneurs is the influence of trauma and insecurity. In the course of interviews I am surprised at how often the people lost their fathers at a young age. Interviewees also describe other forms of financial insecurity, such as bankruptcy. Of 34 first-generation entrepreneurs, *at least* ten experienced significant trauma and insecurity. I later find out that other researchers have found high rates of 'death, separation, inadequacy or rejection of a natural father' among entrepreneurs.

I don't specifically ask my interviewees about trauma and insecurity. Moreover, they don't make much of it. The fact usually arises in passing, as when Andrew Kelly, for example, is describing his experience of working in a milk bar and doing paper runs.

'Did your parents own and run the milk bar?' I ask.

'Yeah,' he replies. 'It was my mother on her own. My father died when I was quite young.' Immediately he resumes his account of doing the paper runs.

Similarly, I ask Gerry Harvey, a billionaire retailer, about how his parents influenced his business career.

'Well, my parents were reasonably well off,' he says, 'but when I was about thirteen they went broke.' He doesn't elaborate.

'They were business people, were they?'

'Hotels. Then they went broke, and then we lived in a garage for a number of years — about three or four years. Sure, that had some bearing on me, because I didn't want to live like that. So that would have had some bearing on my desire to succeed in life, because I'd had a reasonable upbringing to, say, thirteen and then I had the poorest of poor from then on.'

The fact that interviewees describe their experience in such passing terms means that the incidence of trauma and insecurity among these people could be much higher. My wife, Sallee McLaren, is a doctor of clinical psychology who specialises in dealing with anxiety and obsessive-compulsive disorders. She finds that these disorders consistently arise as a result of trauma and insecurity. Yet the people who come to see her often have no sense of having suffered a traumatic event. In many instances the story of the trauma only emerges after several consultations. In my interviews I am not asking questions about trauma or insecurity; it is revealing that the issue arises at all.

Trauma and insecurity often close people down. In the case of anxiety disorders, people try to restore order to their world by controlling what happens to them. They often become hyper-vigilant, attempting to anticipate everything that might happen. They apply themselves with determination to secure their safety. They avoid places and situations that they cannot control. In some cases they stop going outside the home. In some cases they 'numb' their emotions through drugs. In some cases they attach their fears to an object or activity. For example, they become terrified of catching a disease and engage in compulsive cleaning rituals, or become terrified of spiders and avoid going anywhere that spiders might be found.

The people I interview obviously did not close down, or retreat from the world. But they *were* hyper-vigilant, alert to threats and opportunities. They attached themselves to their businesses with fierce determination. They singlemindedly applied themselves to achieving financial security. Andrew Kelly, for example, describes his childhood dream: 'I could actually get money and buy something.' Imelda Roche says that she made a decision very early in life that, whatever it took, she was going to become financially self-reliant. Gerry Harvey remarks that he wanted to make a lot of money.

Joe Saragossi, a migrant from the United States who built a fortune through glass merchandising and fabrication, elaborates on this process. Saragossi lost his father when he was five years old, and lived in an orphanage until he was nineteen and joined the army.

'I think if you do lose your father,' he says, 'you tend to realise that you've got no one to back you up and you'd better be good on your own. I think that drives you.'

He recalls being always hungry: 'I always vowed to myself that I'd never be hungry again.'

When Saragossi came to Australia, he worked for a long time as an electrical contractor. He eventually took over his father-in-law's glass import business, 'with the idea that it was for the children'.

'I was looking for security,' he explains, 'because it doesn't matter what you do, there's always someone attacking you along the way. In business, it's like fighting a war. Your competitors are out to get the market, and you have to be able to defend your market. So it becomes more of a game, but a serious game.'

Later Saragossi returns to the subject of security. 'What's the purpose of acquiring wealth?' he asks rhetorically, then answers his own question. 'Mainly you do it for security, in the first place — and you carry on that way.'

The search for security can never be fully satisfied. The three themes — parents who owned their own businesses or were self-employed, the limited role of education, and the influence of trauma and financial insecurity — go a long way in explaining the diverse and often obscure social backgrounds of the super rich. The themes cut across a wide range of individual histories — from the aristocratic Robert Holmes à Court, whose father left the family when he was an infant, to the dirt-poor Kerry Stokes, whose itinerant parents made a living in whatever way they were able.

> 'BY THE TIME THE OTHERS CATCH UP WITH US, WE'LL BE ON TO THE NEXT ONE.'

When Ernie Campbell wrote *The Sixty Rich Families Who Own Australia* in the early 1960s, he looked at more than the impact of family inheritance in passing on wealth and privilege across generations. He also emphasised the influence of monopoly and imperfect competition. Campbell's argument was a reasonable one: many economists have pointed to the role of monopoly and imperfect competition in the amassing of big fortunes.

According to this view, the capitalist economy works in much the same way as the board game 'Monopoly'. Competition is vigorous at first but soon dies away. Wealth becomes increasingly concentrated. The rich are able to use their monopoly over different industries to keep out newcomers. They are also able to use their monopoly to price their goods above costs, reaping windfall gains. The rich get richer, and the poor get poorer.

The most famous luminaries of the Australian Rich Lists, Rupert Murdoch and Kerry Packer, bear out this view. Newspapers were once a competitive industry, with many small proprietors competing with each other for readers and advertisers. Kerry Packer's grandfather — Robert Clyde Packer — and Rupert Murdoch's father — Sir Keith Murdoch — secured an ownership stake in the industry

Self-made

during the 1920s and 1930s, at a time when the costs of production were rising rapidly. The rising costs meant that small newspaper proprietors fell by the wayside, and newcomers (such as Imelda Roche's father in the 1950s) found it more difficult to enter the business. The media industry became highly concentrated. Moreover, the remaining players, including Robert Clyde Packer's son Frank and Rupert Murdoch, dominated entry into radio and television, which was based on government licences. Television in particular was a licence to make money. The media industry enjoyed high rates of return on investment, protected by limited competition. Rupert Murdoch and Kerry Packer both used their inheritance to build much bigger fortunes.

Economists have spent a lot of time poring over the American, British and Australian Rich Lists, looking precisely at the influence (or otherwise) of monopoly and imperfect competition in the making of big money. The most interesting thing about the lists from the economist's point of view is that the majority of the fortunes in all these lists — in Australia, about three-quarters of the fortunes — were put together in competitive industries. In this respect, the Murdoch and Packer family fortunes are not typical. And the people I interview overwhelmingly had their beginnings in competitive industries, teeming with small businesses. Imelda Roche sold home-manufactured television lamps door-to-door. Bob Clifford struggled in the fishing business. Andrew Kelly sold car radios at the weekend markets. And so on.

Consider Bob Clifford more closely. He started off as a small operator in the fishing industry. 'We struggled in that business for about five years, because we didn't really know the business,' he says. Clifford used his capital from fishing to become a ferryboat operator. Then he used his capital from ferryboats to become a boatbuilder. The shipbuilding industry in Australia was once dominated by Australia's biggest company BHP, supported by large government bounties. The bounties did not save the BHP shipyards. Clifford built his business in spite of cutbacks to government bounties. 'It encouraged us to get more and more efficient each year, as the subsidy was reduced,' he explains. There are big barriers to entry in the shipbuilding industry, but these barriers do not explain Bob Clifford's fortune before the business stumbled.

Economists generally explain big fortunes in competitive industries as a result of disequilibrium in competitive markets. The Austrian economist Joseph Schumpeter put the idea of disequilibrium in eloquent terms in the 1920s when he described the capitalist process as a 'gale of creative destruction'. Schumpeter emphasised the role of entrepreneurs in whipping up the gale. Entrepreneurs were innovators. They did something different, creating disequilibrium in markets. 'First-in' producers had a 'first-mover' advantage: they were unconstrained by competition from established producers. By doing something different, entrepreneurs could charge well above costs and make big profits. They could also grow their business quickly. Entrepreneurs were able to build a fortune before other producers moved to take advantage of the extraordinary profits, and before the market adjusted.

The most obvious way of creating disequilibrium conditions is through the invention or application of a new technology. Bob Clifford is an outstanding example of this process. He leapfrogged old ferry technologies, producing a craft that — in the words of Alistair Mant's book *Intelligent Leadership* — has the capability of transforming the economics of certain kinds of ferry routes. Clifford's high-speed catamarans offered an advantage where quick turnaround was more important than huge payloads. Clifford emphasises the extent to which he still has to stay ahead of the competition. 'By the time the others catch up with us, we'll be on to the next one, if you like.'

Innovation is not only technological, it is also sociological. People change their habits and behaviours for social reasons, such as persuasion, prestige and conformity. 'Most of the disposable income in this world is not disposed of on what people need,' says Brett Blundy, 'but on what they feel they want.' He has a fortune to prove it.

Imelda Roche's natural cosmetics, for example, were not grounded in technical innovation. On the contrary, the products were grounded in the traditional medicine of the long-living Hunza people of the Himalayan mountains. Roche anticipated changing attitudes towards natural products and skin care — and huge growth in the sales of such products in the 1980s and 1990s.

Innovation is also uneven. Disequilibrium conditions occur through uneven development between different regions. Many of the people I interview describe how they observed innovations in other societies, mostly in North America and Western Europe, and then applied the innovations in Australia. One interviewee, for example, describes the effect of his first visit to the United States in the 1950s. He could not believe the productivity levels in the Californian manufacturing plants. 'Their production was much better than ours, *and* their marketing,' he explains. 'While we were the leaders here by far, we became the super leaders — in one year!'

Andrew Kelly is emphatic about the influence of overseas examples from the early 1980s. 'All the way along, I've always travelled over to the US, Europe. Always gone to other retailers, looked and learnt.

'We go over there now and we say, "We could do this better, we could do that better." We do it better and then they do it better, so we're always learning.'

Gerry Harvey says of the process of copying and adapting ideas from overseas: 'Not many of us are pioneers or original thinkers ...

so basically what you're doing is going out and doing something that someone else does, but you do it better.'

Innovation and disequilibrium also go a long way in explaining the diverse and often obscure social backgrounds of the super rich. The old rich tend to be found in established industries and markets. Entrepreneurs on the make gravitate towards new industries and markets — such as shopping centres in the 1970s, gambling in the 1980s, and telecommunications and the internet in the 1990s. Andrew Kelly, for one, reflects that he has not been much troubled by 'old money' in his line of business.

'Fortunately,' he says, 'there's no old money in the car radio business. There's no old money in the mobile phone business, bar a few. Of course, there was when the other networks came in. But by that time the market was very advanced.'

By that time, Kelly had made his fortune.

Chapter Three

A better life

Secrets of the super rich

> 'I WORKED LIKE A SLAVE. EVEN NOW, I DON'T SLEEP MORE THAN THREE OR FOUR HOURS.'

As usual, I begin the interview by asking about the Rich Lists. I ask David Rubin (not his real name) whether there are any groups omitted from the lists. He thinks there are. He thinks 'the foreigners' get special attention in being included, but doesn't know why. He suggests that it might be 'because of this girl who wrote the book'.

Rubin is talking about Ruth Ostrow, a finance journalist for *Business Review Weekly* in the 1980s. (She went on to write a column on sex and relationships for a Sydney tabloid newspaper, and another book entitled *Burning Urges: Australia's Sexual Fantasies*. Money and sex — from one taboo to another.) Ostrow interviewed many of the high-fliers in the 1980s, people reaching public awareness through high-profile takeovers and the Rich Lists. In particular, she interviewed many of the new immigrant entrepreneurs.

Ostrow used her interviews as the basis for the book to which Rubin refers. Entitled *The New Boy Network: Taking Over Corporate Australia*, it was about the 'surprising number of immigrants among our business doyens, many of whom arrived from concentration camps or from war-torn countries and pulled themselves up from nothing to the top rungs of business'. The book featured sketches of

Robert Holmes à Court and Bruno Grollo on the front cover. On the back cover, the blurb declared: 'If you want to know who's *really* running the country, this is the book for you.'

Rubin comments that Ostrow was a foreign girl herself and speaks several foreign languages. 'It was easier for her, at the time, to get closer to the foreign people.' Rubin is referring to Ostrow's Jewish-European background.

No doubt Ostrow's background helped her get interviews with Jewish and immigrant entrepreneurs. I have found in my own research that Australian-born entrepreneurs are more willing to talk with me than immigrant entrepreneurs. In some interviews with immigrant entrepreneurs the fact that the conversation is conducted in English limits their fluency and their depth. Culture makes a difference.

I ask Rubin about his upbringing. He tells me that he was born in Eastern Europe of Jewish parents. His father's side of the family was 'comfortable'. His mother's side was 'quite comfortable'. They were small business people. He left home when he was fourteen — his father sent him away in the hope that he would survive the Holocaust. Rubin describes in a matter-of-fact way how his parents and grandparents on both sides died in a concentration camp.

I feel terribly upset by Rubin's story. I think it is the way he tells it in such a matter-of-fact tone. My own son is twenty years old and still lives at home. I cannot imagine what it must be like to leave home at fourteen years, surrounded by such danger. Nor can I imagine what it must be like to lose parents and siblings in such circumstances. I know that Rubin has had many years in which to come to terms with these events, but I wonder how even that is possible.

I ask him about how the experience affected his business career. He struggles for the words to express himself and I wish I could

Secrets of the super rich

speak in his native language. He describes a scene in which he was standing beside a road, about to cross it. He saw a uniform; the uniform didn't bother him. 'I said to myself, "I know he's a Nazi. He does not know who I am." I compared myself to a dog. When a dog crosses the road, he looks left and right. The same applied to me.

'So, automatically you become more ... alert is the word. Correct?'

Alert is the correct word. Rubin was the prey. He could see the hunter, but the hunter could not see him. Trauma made him hyper-vigilant. He became alert to threats and opportunities. He became a different person from the person he would have become if his life had not been changed by the Holocaust.

At the end of the war Rubin came to Australia. I ask him about his first impressions.

'Something terrible!' he declares. 'The bread was just a white bread with no taste; and tea and milk. That was all. There was no coffee. The accommodation — it was shocking. The heat nearly killed me!'

There was a black market on street corners, just as in Europe. Australians were suspicious of 'foreigners'. He recalls everyone turning in a tram to look at two Polish girls talking in their own language. 'I don't think we were as welcome as people expected,' he says.

Rubin joined another Holocaust survivor in setting up his own business. He tells me how he 'worked like a slave', from early in the morning to late at night. 'Even now,' he says, 'I don't sleep more than three or four hours.'

I ask whether he has slept so little for his whole life. My mind goes back to the Holocaust. I wonder whether he has had a good night's sleep since the Holocaust. He does not answer directly. He simply emphasises that he was driven by his business.

'That's the truth,' he says. 'The business drives you, if you are a responsible person.'

I ask Rubin how he explains his business success. 'I must stress very strongly,' he replies, 'that it was not me, but the people who worked with me ... That's the secret in business. I can have any idea, any vision, but somebody's got to do it. Somebody's got to roll up their sleeves and do it.'

I press Rubin further about his own role. He struggles again for the words, then says, 'I'm a creator ... I definitely had vision. But don't forget, Michael, it was easy to have vision when nothing was available here. So don't think that I'm a genius.

'I went, for example, to a [trade] exhibition in Paris and I came home with a new idea. Before the opposition woke up to it, we had already made money. We were established on it.'

Rubin's vision allowed him to take advantage of uneven development between regions of the world — to take ideas and products from Europe and apply them to Australia, breaking new ground and reaping big gains. I ask him whether his competitors were resentful. 'Competitors?' he says. 'I didn't see any competitors. They saw me. It's true, think about it. When you're doing well and you're successful, you don't see the competitors — they see you. No, I didn't see any competitors.'

Most questions Rubin answers without comment. There's a few, though, on which he is more sensitive. I ask him whether he would describe himself as a religious person, and then ask him, 'What is the role of religion in business life?' I'm always self-conscious when I ask Jewish interviewees this question, loaded as it is with the memory of the Holocaust.

Rubin is alert to this question, with good reason. 'I noticed that in your questionnaire,' he says. Then he replies that he is observant, not

Secrets of the super rich

religious; adding, 'It's my club. Is that an answer?... Where else can I go? To the Melbourne Club? No, despite being here for so many years.'

There have been complaints made about the Melbourne Club regarding its discrimination against Jews. Rubin is not the first Jewish entrepreneur to mention the Club.

He continues, 'Yes, I do go to the synagogue. Outside there I meet friends — but I've got no friends left. But I *used* to meet friends. I used to talk; it helped.

'I saw that question, yes. It does help to belong somewhere, not only for my own sake but for my wife's sake and our children's sake. I don't know what others have answered you. But is it important? *Yes*. You've got to belong somewhere, and the children have got to know that they belong somewhere.'

At the end of the interview I ask Rubin if there is anything he wants to add to what he has already said.

'I'd only want to add,' he says, 'that Australia is a wonderful country, one of the best countries in the world.' He is very sincere in this. 'There is no freedom for a migrant like that in Australia. If he wants to excel, the opportunity is here — it's up to him. I'm proud of Australia. Australia has done a lot for me. I'm hopefully classified as an honest citizen and a grateful person. That's all I have to say. And I repeat again — the best country in which to bring up children is Australia.'

> **'YOU WORK AND YOU SAVE, AND THAT IS HOW YOU BECOME SOMEONE.'**

Most immigrants in the nineteenth and early twentieth centuries came from the British Isles — English, Scottish, Welsh and Irish people. The great cultural and social division in Australian society during this era was between the English and Scottish Protestants on the one hand and the Irish Catholics on the other.

There are shadows of this division in many of my interviews. One Jewish man, for example, recalls arriving in Australia in the 1960s.

'I went out with a girl once who said to me, "You're not Catholic, are you?"'

'I said, "No, I'm Jewish."'

'She said, "Oh, that's okay. As long as you're not Catholic, I'll go out with you."'

'I thought, what a wonderful country, they don't hate the Jews!'

In the wake of World War II, Australian politicians warned that Australia must 'populate or perish'. The government embarked on a massive migration program. At first it tried to draw most of its immigrants from Britain. When this was not possible, it extended the net to 'displaced people' from eastern Europe — such as David Rubin. During the 1950s and 1960s the net extended to southern Europe, in particular Italy, Greece and Yugoslavia. In the 1970s the Whitlam Labor Government removed the White Australia Policy, opening the door to Asian migrants. By the 1980s more migrants were coming from Asia than from anywhere else. In the 1990s governments wound back migration, but by then migration had transformed the society. Australia was now one of the most ethnically diverse societies in the world — perhaps *the* most ethnically diverse society in the world.

In the 1970s social scientists observed that migrants of non-English-speaking background often came from rural, low-skilled backgrounds. They were disadvantaged on account of social class, migration and language. They did the jobs that the locals did not want for themselves. They were concentrated in the low-paid, low-skilled jobs — the 'factory fodder' jobs. Their children had reached their maturity at the end of the 'long boom' which had brought migrants to Australia in the first place. There was good reason to believe that migrants were locked into a disadvantaged position in Australian society.

From the 1980s a new wave of research came up with some surprising results. The children of migrants were disproportionately successful in terms of educational achievement and professional occupation. One study observed, for example, that children of non-English-speaking background were disproportionately likely to stay on for their Higher School Certificate, notwithstanding relatively low IQ scores (reflecting language difficulties) and low socio-economic background.

From the start, migrants were also prominent in the Rich Lists. The company raiders of the 1980s — including Robert Holmes à Court, Alan Bond and Ronald Brierley — were mostly migrants. In 1991, in the wake of the company raiders, the proportion of overseas-born among the individuals and families on the Rich Lists was still much higher (at 30 per cent) than the proportion of overseas born among the total Australian population (22 per cent). Since then the proportion of migrants on the list has fallen (to 23 percent). Even so, it is still the case that notwithstanding the disadvantages of migration, migrants are no less likely to accumulate large fortunes than those who were born in Australia.

A few of the migrants on the Rich Lists were already rich when they came to Australia. The New Zealand-born company raider Ron Brierley moved to Sydney in the late 1960s to extend the span of his share raiding activities. The Taiwanese property developer Hsien-Ta Fu moved to Brisbane in 1992 under a business migration scheme, in order to escape political uncertainties in Taiwan. It is revealing, though, that both men came from modest backgrounds. Brierley was the son of a public servant; Fu was the son of a street vendor. They were men who had crashed through local class and status systems. They were men on the move. They moved to Australia.

A better life

More commonly, migrants on the Rich Lists arrived with little in their pockets. We know this because many of them worked for wages in low-wage, low-skill jobs on their arrival, or alternatively they were self-employed. Carlo Valmorbida worked in a factory. Jack and Chaim Liberman carted clothing rejects and offcuts from factories for resale. Frank Lowy was a factory operative and drove a delivery van. Larry Adler drove a taxi. As soon as they were able to, they established their own businesses.

Nick Balagiannis, for example, tells me how he grew up in a small mountain town in Greece. His father worked for the government as a forest ranger. Balagiannis left school at the age of fifteen and found work in a small factory. Then he went to Athens, where he was a waiter for several years. In 1965, at the age of seventeen, he migrated to Melbourne, where he worked as a kitchen hand and a cook for his brother-in-law. Then he found work as a butcher in the abattoirs. Migrants, he reflects, are willing to do anything to make it better: 'You're not choosy at the beginning, or even later.

'You work and you save, and that is how you become someone.'

Balagiannis went on to lease a coffee shop in inner-city Melbourne, and then an amusement parlour on the city outskirts. I ask what gave him the idea of having his own business.

'When you work for yourself,' he replies, 'you definitely make more money, *if* you're successful ... It gives you that advantage. You work longer hours, but you control what time you work. You give yourself the orders.'

Balagiannis started repairing the pinball machines used at his amusement parlour. Then he began assembling machines for sale. 'I started under the house,' he recalls. 'I was importing the parts and I was making the cabinets locally, and so I put them together. That's how I started the first manufacturing.

'The pinballs ... I used to deliver them myself. Sometimes the wife would give us a hand to put them on the truck. That's how I started, you know.'

From pinball machines Balagiannis diversified into poker machines. He recalls seeing the first electronic poker machines. 'I saw those machines and I knew what they did wrong. So I thought that I would start again. Make my own design, and this and that, and put my own experience in — and here we go!'

I comment that not many manufacturing businesses were starting up in the 1980s.

'I was in a good industry, actually,' he responds. 'The entertainment industry was a good industry. It had growth.'

The entertainment industry had growth, the gambling industry had huge growth. New fortunes were made in growth industries.

> **'THE MORE INTERESTING QUESTION, WHICH YOU CAN'T ASK, IS: "WHICH GROUPS DIDN'T MAKE IT?"'**

I ask one Australian-born man what he thinks about the high profile of immigrants on the Rich Lists.

'I think it's entirely what you'd expect,' he replies. 'The most energetic people are the last people off the boat or the plane. It's that immigrant energy that comes through all the time.

'The more interesting question, which you can't ask, is: "Which groups didn't make it?" It's not at all surprising that the list has a number of nationalities there that are new.'

The people I interview consistently affirm the force of immigrant energy. They emphasise that migrants work very, very hard. Migrants are also hungry for success, prepared to live a 'mean life' in the present in order to achieve a better life in the future. At the same time, there is a common reluctance to press beyond this observation and explore the disproportionate success of particular ethnic groups. In his book *The Wealth and Poverty of Nations*, the American economic historian David Landes commented that 'if we can learn anything from the history of economic development, it is that culture makes a difference'. The enterprise of expatriate communities in different societies — the Chinese in East and Southeast Asia, the Lebanese in West Africa, the Jews and Calvinists throughout much of Europe, and so on — bears witness to the influence of culture. Yet the subject, Landes observed, frightens scholars. 'It has a sulfuric odor of race and inheritance, an air of immutability.'

Scholars avoid the subject because they fear making judgements that some cultures are 'better' in some respects than others — that they are more effective for particular purposes. They fear making judgements of this sort because such judgements in the past justified a view of some ethnic groups and cultures as 'superior' or 'inferior' to others. In turn, racial ideologies promoted policies of discrimination and even extermination, from the 'stolen generation' among the Aboriginal people of Australia to the Nazi death camps and the Holocaust. What happened once can happen again: best to leave the subject alone — or adopt a view that 'stereotypes' of any kind are racist.

It is not just scholars who are frightened by the issue. *BRW* skirts around it in relation to the Rich Lists. It celebrates the influence of migrants. It lists the many different countries from which they came. Migrants on the Rich Lists came from all over Europe, especially the former Eastern Bloc countries such as Poland and Hungary. They came from North America. They came from the Asia-Pacific region, including China, Papua New Guinea and New Zealand. They came from the Mediterranean, including Greece, Lebanon and Israel. They came from Southern Africa.

Secrets of the super rich

But beyond this point, *BRW* is less forthcoming. We are on sensitive ground. In fact, there is less ethnic diversity in the Rich Lists than first seems to be the case. Above all, Jewish entrepreneurs are extraordinarily prominent in the lists. They include some of the wealthiest individuals in Australia. Of the eleven billionaire listings in 2001 (nine individuals and two families), six are Jewish. They include Frank Lowy (second-richest individual after Kerry Packer), Richard Pratt (third-richest) and the Smorgon family (the richest family). Jews account for more than one-half of the immigrant fortunes. Many of them (including Lowy and Pratt) were refugees from the Holocaust.

Otherwise, entrepreneurs are overwhelmingly drawn from English-speaking countries (such as Britain, the United States and South Africa); the Mediterranean (Italy, Greece and Lebanon); and the Overseas Chinese (from Asia and the Pacific).

Most of the people I interview are uneasy about this issue — on account of the shadow of the Holocaust. One Australian-born man of British ancestry queries me when I ask about 'ethnic patterns' in the new economy. 'It's almost a racist question,' he says dubiously.

A Jewish interviewee observes that anti-semitism has 'gone down unbelievably' around the world. 'But you know what?' he adds. 'It also sparks up very fast. Whenever there is a recession, the rich and the elite are always subjected to punishment. Invariably, Jews are singled out in that regard.'

Another Jewish man — the Australian-born son of a migrant, whom I will call Daniel Ginsberg — cautiously comments that I am 'leading to a very interesting area' in asking about ethnicity. He turns the question back on me. 'What is the predominant ethnic or religious background of the people on the Rich List other than Anglo-Saxon?' he asks.

I reply that it is Jewish.

'Why is that?' Ginsberg asks.

I say that it is a huge issue. It's a safe answer.

He enlarges on my comment. 'It's fascinating and scary,' he says, 'because of the whole persecution thing in the twentieth century as a result of commercial success. And that's a very scary thing.'

At the end of the interview Ginsberg returns to the issue. 'I'm concerned ... if you're going to mention that the predominant non-Anglo-Saxon members of the list are Jewish. I'm concerned about whether it's going to be mentioned, I'm concerned about that. I don't know whether I should be or I shouldn't be. It's a sensitive issue for Jewish people.'

The prominence of Jewish entrepreneurs is one of the most striking aspects of the Rich Lists. It is certainly the most interesting aspect of the migrant profile on the lists. And I don't see how I can avoid exploring this issue: it lies at the heart of my project. It exemplifies the fact that wealth accumulation is not an abstract economic process, it's a social process, a cultural process. Culture makes a difference in wealth accumulation. It makes a difference, for example, on account of the values that are instilled in children in the course of growing up. Similarly, it makes a difference in terms of the social networks that are available to people for advice, support and inspiration.

I tell Ginsberg that I don't see how I can avoid the issue. I also say that Jewish economic success is an 'extraordinary achievement', something of which to be proud. Maybe my comment is banal. Perhaps it is simply the product of growing up in the Australian suburbs, rather than under the shadow of the Holocaust. Certainly Ginsberg is not convinced that I've grasped what is at stake.

'But it's religion, you know,' he says urgently. 'It's what's in your head.

'I suppose it's what is in your head and your heart that makes you. I'm concerned. I recognise that you're going to mention it. I'm concerned about it and I hope there's no backlash from it. You need to treat it delicately.'

> **'PEOPLE WERE QUITE SETTLED IN THEIR COMFORTABLE LIVES. THEY WANTED TO BE LEFT IN PEACE.'**

The same themes that apply to entrepreneurs generally — and that account for their diverse social backgrounds — apply no less to migrants' fortunes. Migrant entrepreneurs overwhelmingly came from small business backgrounds; their vehicle for mobility was small business. Education was overwhelmingly irrelevant. The migration experience itself was often traumatic, or was the outcome of trauma. Migrants made their money in growth industries, often drawing on their overseas knowledge. As David Rubin bluntly states, 'it was easy to have vision when nothing was available here'.

These themes apply in different ways for different ethnic groups. Ethnic groups carried their own distinctive cultural and historical baggage when they arrived in Australia. They brought different experiences, skills, habits and values. This is why migrants from some ethnic groups were more likely to accumulate great fortunes than those from other ethnic groups.

For example, some ethnic groups — notably Jews, Chinese and Lebanese — had a long history as 'middle person minorities', operating small businesses in competitive industries. Jews, for instance, worked in the garment industry in medieval Spain, the Ottoman Empire, the Russian Empire, and the New World, including Australia. When Jewish refugees arrived in Melbourne in the 1930s and 1940s, many found their way into the 'rag trade'. In his memoirs

'Flinders Lane...Memory Lane', one veteran of the trade, Robert Salter, says: 'The reason why so many Jewish migrants were involved in that kind of business was, of course, that not much capital was required to start. Also, they were mainly tailors and dressmakers in Europe and could practically set up business with one or two sewing machines which could be bought on time-payment.'

Jewish entrepreneurs who had their beginnings in the Melbourne rag trade included Jack and Chaim Lieberman, Abe Goldberg, Marc Besen, John Gandel, Solomon Lew, Nathan Baran and Joseph Gutnick.

In more specific terms, immigrants had often owned their own businesses or were self-employed in their country of origin. Their parents and grandparents had owned their own businesses. Friends, networks and communal associations further encouraged them in setting up their own businesses. Small businesses in competitive industries encouraged habits of hard work, long hours, careful spending and commercial reliability. One Jewish interviewee emphasises the importance of 'watching my father, knowing his history, his background; watching my friends'.

Take, for example, Isador Magid. Magid's grandparents came from Siberia. They settled near Harbin, a city in Manchuria in the north of China. The grandfather was an innkeeper; Magid's father was an accountant with his own business. Magid escaped from Manchuria to Shanghai (ahead of the Japanese invasion), and then to Australia. He recalls the arrival of the Communists in Shanghai. 'When the Communists came in, they made it very clear that there was nothing for business people to do. It was a Communist regime. They didn't need any intermediaries or anybody else. You could see that your chapter was closed.'

One chapter closed, another began. Magid began a succession of businesses in Australia. First he exploited his existing business connections in China, importing goats hair and furs. 'It was complicated and not very profitable,' he recalls. 'We led a very modest life.' Next he bought a popcorn factory. It almost sent him broke. Then he started land development, subdivision and building activity on a very small scale, encouraged by the suburban growth he saw around him. He had no previous experience of the industry.

'None at all,' Magid says emphatically. 'None at all. In China, you couldn't do those things, you just couldn't.'

He recalls his 'great trepidation' as he invested money in his first subdivision. It was successful. 'From there, we took big steps and started developing bigger and bigger chunks of land.'

I ask Magid how he explains his success, given his initial lack of experience. He embarks on the story of his most ambitious land subdivision of all, in the southeastern suburbs of Melbourne. In the first instance, he says, he saw the opportunity in terms of the complete disparity between the number of workers in the area and the lack of local housing. 'Thousands of people worked there. General Motors was in this boom, so was International Harvester, and H. J. Heinz. All those big factories were there, and there was no housing at all.

'So I thought, well, this is the place where people must want to live across the road from their jobs. They'd save so much time, they'd save so much money. They wouldn't need to have a car.'

Then Magid describes how he was able to act on his insight. First he faced dogged resistance from local landowners, municipal authorities and the State government. 'People were quite settled in their comfortable lives. They wanted to be left in peace.' But he persisted and ultimately prevailed. He recalls his delight when he obtained an interview with Sir Henry Bolte, Premier of Victoria, who intervened in a rezoning dispute on his behalf. 'I thought, what a beautiful country when an ordinary migrant, unknown to anybody, can reach the Premier of the State he lives in.

'In China they wouldn't dream of it. You can't get to the big person there and talk to him like a human being, like an equal man.'

Magid learned his skills in an uncertain and often hostile environment. In Australia his talents flourished. Culture makes a difference, but so does environment. Other migrant interviewees also acknowledge the role of economic freedom and opportunity in Australia, notwithstanding instances of prejudice and resentment.

'There is no freedom for a migrant like that in Australia,' David Rubin says. 'If he wants to excel, the opportunity is here — it's up to him.'

Ethnic groups brought longstanding traditions, habits and values when they arrived in Australia. They also carried more specific experiences — the circumstances of their migration. Many Jewish migrants were fuelled by the trauma of the Holocaust. They had endured chronic insecurity and abject humiliation. They had often lost their families, but they had survived. They were, to use the words of David Rubin, alert and driven — alert to threats and opportunities, driven to overcome their insecurity and humiliation.

The effects of trauma and insecurity were a consistent theme in Ruth Ostrow's interviews with migrant entrepreneurs in the 1980s. In Ostrow's book *The New Boy Network*, the property developer Ervin Graf, for example, described life on the run in the 1940s, first from the Nazis and then from the Russians, and his state of mind at the end of the war. 'I had adapted to the loss.

> 'IT'S ALMOST LIKE SOMEBODY WHO CAME TO EARTH FROM A PLANET DOUBLE THE MASS OF EARTH WOULD BE TWICE AS STRONG AS YOU OR ME.'

During the war it just doesn't matter. You become nonchalant. We walked through dead bodies. There were hundreds in the streets.'

Graf recalled working from 6 am to 8 pm seven days a week on his arrival in Australia.

'Migrants try to prove they are as good as the next one,' he explained. 'Their background aggravates this need. We arrived without anything. No security. We wanted security but also to overcome the humiliation of being treated as subhumans.'

One of the people I interviewed — I will call him Jared Cohen — reflects on the effect of the Holocaust on his father. Wealth accumulation, he remarks, 'goes back to basic insecurity — the insecurity of the individual, the insecurity based on the background'. Insecurity is 'an unbelievable driver for performance'.

'I can't tell you some of the things my father has done to survive,' he says. 'They came to a country like Australia where the work ethic was not what it is today, where survival instincts weren't required. It was just a matter of coming from another environment.'

The survivors of the Holocaust, Cohen elaborates, 'were living in the equivalent of a different gravity'. His father's experience was completely different from that of the people he was competing with when he got here. 'It's almost like somebody who came to Earth from a planet double the mass of Earth would be twice as strong as you or me and could physically overwhelm and overpower us, or lift things twice the [normal] weight, because they've been living in a different gravity.

'They might be the same size, but their muscles will be twice as developed, because they've been living in a different gravity.'

Jill Margo's biography of Frank Lowy — *Frank Lowy: Pushing the Limits* — also highlights the influence of the Holocaust, alongside other themes in the success of migrant entrepreneurs. Lowy was born in 1930 and grew up in a small town in the southern part of Czechoslovakia. His father was a commercial traveller; his mother operated a small grocery shop, with help from her children. In 1942 the general roundup of Jews meant that his mother's family in nearby Slovakia was taken away. Lowy's parents thereupon moved to Budapest, the capital of Hungary, where they hoped to blend in among the larger population. Here Lowy attended school, but was an indifferent student.

In 1943 Lowy's father was detained by secret police, who sent him to a Hungarian concentration camp. In turn, the remaining family separated in order to increase their chances of survival. Lowy, thirteen years old at the time, remained with his mother and increasingly took charge of their survival. He spent much of his time on the streets, trying to get food and information.

'I don't know how,' he told Margo, 'but I kept on finding food. During this period we grew very close, relying on each other to stay alive. I went through many of life's experiences in a very short space of time — living, dying, being scared, afraid ...

'Once father was taken away my childhood ended. I was never a child again. In a sense I became more like a father to my mother. My days were spent scheming about how to live, eat and survive. I was always listening to what was said to make sure we could survive.'

Lowy's father died at Auschwitz. The rest of the family survived. After the war, Lowy followed one of his brothers to Palestine. He fought in the Israeli War of Independence as a teenager, but then in 1952 followed his sister and mother to Sydney. His first job was in a toolmaking factory. 'The job was demoralising,' he recalled. 'I'd get up at 6 am, catch the bus, go to the factory with my sandwiches in my little bag, be bored out of my mind all day, then come home.

Secrets of the super rich

I started on the grinding machine and soon became assistant storeman, where absolutely nothing was required of me.'

By 1954 Lowy had found work as a delivery truck driver for a smallgoods manufacturer. In the course of this job he met John Saunders (then John Schwartz), a Hungarian Jew who owned a delicatessen at Sydney's Town Hall railway station. Like Lowy, Saunders was a survivor of the Holocaust who had come to Australia to get as far away as possible from Europe. He had spent the war years in concentration camps, ending up at Auschwitz.

The two men became friendly and decided to go into business together. They opened a delicatessen in Blacktown on the western outskirts of Sydney, where there was a large immigrant population from Europe whose tastes in food were not met by local businesses. The shop, Saunders recalled, did fantastic business. 'The new Australians in Blacktown were very good customers. While Australians used to buy sixpence worth of devon and a shilling's worth of ham, the new Australians bought salami by the yard.'

Lowy applied his alertness, discipline and determination to business. He was always looking for new opportunities. He was always taking the next step. Margo constantly refers to his hyper-vigilance and persistence. He was 'hellbent on achieving security,' she observed, and 'single-minded in his determination to be successful'.

'I have this force within that constantly drives me to improve, not necessarily for financial gain but for being able to do more,' Lowy reflected. 'Although my belly is full I am still hungry. I can't sit around and do nothing. My mind just doesn't rest, whether it's five o'clock in the morning or at midnight, I still give all I have to everything I do.'

First the partners opened a coffee shop. Then they subdivided land. Then they built shops, following the example of Ervin Graf, another

A better life

Holocaust survivor. Graf was building his own shops nearby Lowy and Saunders' delicatessen. He recalled visiting the delicatessen. 'I said to Lowy and Saunders, "two smart boys like you should go into investment and building," and that is exactly what they did.'

Then the pair built a shopping centre, having heard of this retail industry phenomenon sweeping the United States. They were among the first to introduce shopping centres in Australia. The business grew rapidly and Lowy regularly visited the United States for ideas. He approached American managers for permission to tour their centres. 'Once they found out that we were from Australia, the Americans were remarkably open and helpful,' Lowy recalled. 'They were proud of their achievements and shared their knowledge freely.' After a while, though, Lowy no longer wanted extended tours — it was too time-consuming. He did his own research.

In the United States, shopping centres were often built at the intersections of major freeway systems. They were big and sprawling. Lowy and Saunders adapted the arrangement to Australian conditions, building shopping centres in the suburbs, often close to railway lines. The land was relatively expensive, requiring more efficient use of space — for example, smaller shops and multi-level car parks.

From the 1970s on Lowy and Saunders expanded their business to the States, the home of shopping centres. Their Australian experience now gave them a competitive edge, as they were able to squeeze more value from the same space than local US developers could. By the 1990s the American outpost had outstripped the Australian empire. The group also straddled other parts of the globe.

Lowy, Margo observed, was a man who needed 'not only to get to the top of the mountain but to own it, too — and to own large armies that can defend it from others'. Then again, 'for him the reality is that the top can never be seen'. As he approached the top, another peak came into view — and then another, and another. There were always new threats; there were always new opportunities. It was always necessary to keep pushing for the top.

All of the familiar themes are found in Lowy's story: a family background in small business; the limited role of education; trauma and insecurity; and innovation in Australia and the United States. Yet the Holocaust casts the longest shadow in the story, driving Lowy forward in his search for security — as it did many others.

Chapter Four

Driven

> 'I FOUND THAT MY MIND HAS BEEN GOING 150 MILES AN HOUR ALL ITS LIFE. IT'S HARD TO SLOW IT DOWN.'

Clive Berghofer's father was a labourer, among other things, who finished up as a small farmer just outside Toowoomba in southern Queensland. Berghofer junior attended the local school, where there were sixteen children from preparatory to grade seven.

'I hated school,' he recalls. 'I'm dyslexic. I like work. I hated school. I was good at arithmetic, but I just hated English, geography and history. I'm a terrible speller, I'm a terrible writer and a terrible reader.'

It is typical that Berghofer declares his love of work in the same breath as he declares his hatred of school. Indeed, there is one recurring theme in this interview: he believes in work. 'Well, work,' he says a moment later, 'I love work. When I was twelve I could outwork any man, you know.'

Berghofer left school at thirteen. He remembers with pride that even as a kid he used to go out sewing bags. 'At fourteen,' he says, 'I could sew more bags than anybody. I could sew record numbers of bags. I could sew them properly.

'Then I got a job in a sawmill. They'd only work 40-odd hours. Then I used to cut firewood of an afternoon and that. I used to buy firewood from the farmers for ten shillings, I think it was, and then sell it for fifteen shillings a load or something.'

Later he became a carpenter's labourer. 'They only worked 40 hours too. They didn't get overtime then. So in the afternoon, as soon as I knocked off work, I'd have a job down the road and I might work at it well into the night, or I might race in early of a morning and work. You know, I didn't start [the day job] until eight o'clock.

'Then at weekends, I'd work all weekend. Then holidays — say the Show Day holiday — my mates would say, "We're going to the Show." They might have only been paid £2 or £3 a day in those days, but then they might have gone to the Show and spent £5, say. Righto, I used to work for the day. I may have made £3 or £4, plus I probably saved £5 because I didn't go to the Show. And I just gradually built up my money.'

Stating the obvious, I remark, 'So you've always worked pretty hard.'

'It's common sense,' he replies. 'See, a lot of people can do things, a lot of people can work hard, but they've got no common sense in doing it. Some people have got the common sense to do it, but they're too bloody lazy to work. But I was lucky — I had the common sense and the ability to work.'

Berghofer tells the story of how he started working on contract. It's clear that when he speaks of common sense, he means not just working hard for wages but working hard on his own account.

'A guy rang me up one day and said, "I want a fowl house built." I said that I charged seven shillings and sixpence an hour.

'He said, "I don't want it by the hour, I want it by the contract."

'I said, "What does contract mean?"

'He said, "You give me a price for the whole fowl house."

'I said, "I've never done this." But I sat down and worked out every nail and every screw. It came to £27 for this fowl house. I allowed two days at £5 a day — and I was only getting about £5 a week then. I thought, holy hell, if I can earn £5 a day I'm going to be rich!

'So he said, "Righto, you can do the job."

'So I went in and I started very early one morning, and I finished with the car lights. I did it in a day and I made £10 in a day. I thought, I'll do more contract work now.'

His father was not impressed when Berghofer started working on his own account. 'My father was brought up in the Depression days,' Berghofer explains. 'They were always frightened of spending money and that. When I was working as a carpenter's labourer, I had that much work lined up — my weekend work — that I said, "I'm going out on my own."

'"Oh, you fool!" he said. "You're getting £8 a bloody week. You're making good money at weekends. You're bloody mad!"

'I said, "After twelve months at this job I'm getting out on my own — you see!" And I got out on my own. Then I said, "I think I'll put someone on. I've got that much work, I think I'll start employing a man."

'"Oh, you bloody fool!"

'But I took no notice of anybody. I said, "Right, if I want to do it, I'll do it." So I started putting a few people on.'

Berghofer went on to make his fortune in property development around Toowoomba. He still regularly works on site. 'I drove the kerb machine this morning,' he says, 'and kerbed a subdivision that we're doing.' I can see by his hands that he's telling the truth.

'I used to work with the crew all the time once, but I don't work with them as much now, unless it is really important and I want to get it done faster. At the shopping centre that I built here, I worked with them the whole time.'

I ask whether there are any personal costs in keeping up this pace of work. At first Berghofer flounders for words. 'Oh no, my health is probably...' He trails off. Then he tries again. 'You know, I've got aching bones and things. Plenty of people have.'

Then he finds an anecdote and is off and away again, telling me how he was the only foreman on the construction site for his shopping centre.

'I designed it and built it myself. I had a back operation in the middle of it. I had a laminectomy halfway through it. The doctor said, "Your back has caved in. Look, the only way you'll fix it is with an operation, but you'll have to be in hospital for seven days and you'll have to be off your feet for six weeks."

'So it was going to be bloody hard for me to work.' I said, "I'll have to do something, because I'm in too much pain."

'I was in hospital, and after four days he came to visit me. I was walking around pretty well. He said, "You're recovering well."

'I said, "Yes, I've got to."

'He said, "When do you want to go home?"

'I said, "I'd better not go home today, I'll go home tomorrow."

'It was five days, and I came back to work.'

I ask Berghofer about his plans for the future. Again he tells me a story. He talks about his marriage breakup, then about the breakup of a more recent relationship.

'I was sitting at home at night time by myself,' he says. 'A person usually has kids at home or somebody, you know, moving around.' His aloneness made his thoughts turn to slowing down, and he decided to prepare a plan for doing so. But next day he went back to work again, 'probably as busy as ever'.

Secrets of the super rich

'I found that my mind has been going 150 miles an hour all its life,' Berghofer says. 'It's hard to slow it down even to 101 miles.

'Some people, they've done nothing much in life and they can retire and potter around the house. With me, I'll do my hedges and mow my whole lawn in about two and a half hours. Some blokes will spend the day doing the bloody hedges, you know.

'Everything I've done I've always done with speed, and so it's hard to say, "Look, I'm going to slow down."'

Berghofer is occasionally vulnerable as he describes his marriage breakup, or life on his own. But he is also irrepressible. He brushes aside his vulnerability, and launches into more anecdotes about the virtues of hard work and the danger of over-education.

'Opportunity doesn't always knock,' he warns. 'Some people say that they only want a full piece of cake. Some people say that half a piece of cake is better than none. I always say any bit of cake is better than none. If opportunity knocks, grab it, because you don't know what it turns into or when the next one is going to turn up.'

At the end of the interview Berghofer tells a joke about a gardener who works at a church in London:

> One day the minister comes along and says that the garden is not big enough to keep the man busy. 'What we want you to do,' he says, 'is to open and close the doors of the church, and write down the names of the people so we've got their names.'
> 'I can't write,' the gardener replies, 'and so I won't be able to write the names down.'
> 'Then I think we'll have to let you leave,' the minister says. 'We'll have to get someone else to do the job.'
> In due course the gardener goes on to open a tobacco shop, and then another, and another. Eventually he has a huge chain of shops. One day he goes to his bank manager, who asks him to fill

in a form. The one-time gardener confesses that he cannot write. 'Holy hell,' the manager says. 'Here you are, you own this huge chain of tobacco shops all through London and you can't write! Where would you be if you could write?'

'Opening and closing the doors to a church,' the man replies.

Berghofer chuckles. He identifies with the gardener. And the gardener had the last laugh.

Economic theory is heavily based upon a model of the individual as self-interested and rational. According to this theory, individuals are guided by self-interest. They are motivated by what the classical economist Adam Smith described as 'the desire for betterment'. Individuals usually look out for themselves. In doing so, they are guided by rational criteria. They consistently choose to do things that they think will provide most benefit at least cost.

This model of human behaviour is correct a good deal of the time. People regularly pursue their own selfish interests. Moreover, it seems to provide a fairly straightforward explanation of wealth accumulation. After all, who doesn't want to be rich? Surely super-wealth is the ultimate form of self-betterment! A few of the people I interview seem to support this type of view. I ask one man what motivated him to keep expanding his business. 'Just greed, I suppose,' he replies in a matter-of-fact way.

Yet there are major limitations in the model of self-interested rational behaviour. It does not take into account culture and society — or in the language of Adam Smith, 'moral sentiments'. Smith

> 'SO I BELIEVE IN THE WHITE ANGLO-SAXON PROTESTANT WORK ETHIC, AND I'M A LIVING EXAMPLE OF IT.'

(unlike many of his intellectual followers) understood that economic motivation is complicated. It is not something that we are born with, it is something that we learn. It is embedded in our culture. Different cultures teach different lessons about self-betterment. They teach different lessons about economic motivation.

The Australian Aboriginals, for example, evolved a culture — over a period of something between 40 000 and 60 000 years — that was focused on social obligations, rather than accumulation. Aboriginals used their surpluses to build extensive social networks grounded in reciprocal obligations. People gave things away — food, artefacts, their children's hand in marriage — in the expectation that the favour would one day be returned.

In his remarkable book *The Future Eaters*, Tim Flannery explains how the emphasis on social obligations was an adaptation to the Australian environment. The climate was unpredictable, resulting in the erratic availability of resources. (As I write these words, there is drought in the southern States of Australia and floods in the northern States.) On this account, extraordinary social obligations sometimes had to be honoured. In the most severe droughts, for example, people temporarily abandoned their land and sought refuge with neighbours. Social obligations were a matter of survival.

It takes extremely strong social bonds for people to share limited resources with guests in difficult times. Aboriginals spent the better part of their time engaged in cultural activities, such as religion and ritual. Religion and ritual underpinned the social obligations. They guaranteed that social obligations would be honoured in the most trying conditions.

In other words, self-betterment does not necessarily result in wealth accumulation. In the case of the Australian Aboriginals, self-betterment involved ongoing redistribution of wealth. No wonder Aboriginals were confused by the culture of the European invaders. No wonder, also, that few Aboriginals show much interest in wealth accumulation two hundred years after the European invasion. There are no Aboriginals on the Rich Lists.

The ways in which we direct our behaviour and improve our social position depend heavily on the culture and society in which we live.

The agricultural revolution — the domestication of plants and animals in the Fertile Crescent of the Middle East about 13 000 years ago — unleashed unprecedented capacity for wealth accumulation. The societies that emerged in the wake of the agricultural revolution have overwhelmingly valued wealth accumulation. At the same time, the German sociologist Max Weber, in a classic study *The Protestant Ethic and the Spirit of Capitalism*, observed that the ways in which societies valued wealth accumulation were not the same. Different societies valued it in different ways.

Weber was trying to explain why the industrial revolution developed in Europe. Following the collapse of the Roman Empire, the countries of Western Europe were a political and economic backwater. Over the next thousand years China, India and the Middle East were all major powers at various times. The Chinese in particular were way ahead of Europe in technological and economic development during this era. Weber argued that from the seventeenth century Western Europe got the break on other civilisations because it developed an entirely new attitude towards wealth accumulation.

Other civilisations valued wealth accumulation on account of the comfort, security, power and pleasure it could bring. In contrast, the first capitalist merchants and industrialists of Western Europe did not want wealth so that they could live a luxurious lifestyle. On the contrary, their lifestyle was self-denying and frugal. They valued hard work, sobriety, thrift, honesty and reliability. Rather than spending their money, they reinvested it to promote further expansion of their enterprises.

Weber called the new attitude towards wealth accumulation 'the spirit of capitalism'. He argued that it arose from the new Protestant religion — in particular, one branch of Protestantism called Puritanism. Puritans believed that luxury was an evil but that hard-earned material success was a sign of God's blessing. Puritan beliefs and values provided the basis for a new type of wealth accumulation. '*Time* is *short*,' warned the seventeenth-century Puritan divine Richard Baxter, 'and *work* is *long*.'

There are echoes of Weber (and Richard Baxter) in all my interviews. Interviewees repeatedly stress the importance of hard work.

Harry Tyrrell recalls: 'I used to work seven days a week, twelve hours a day, for years.'

Imelda Roche quotes her husband: 'In those early years, we worked eight days a week, twenty-five hours a day.'

'It's an awful drug,' says another man, who has made his money in the new economy. 'I suppose I'm one of those people they call a workaholic.'

Interviewees also repeatedly stress the importance of sobriety, thrift, honesty and reliability.

'One of the troubles I have,' Joe Saragossi says ironically, 'is that I'm not interested in racing or gambling or drinking or womanising, and so I don't really have a colourful life to spend my money on.'

Gerry Harvey illustrates his thrift by drawing attention to the shirt he is wearing. It's a T-shirt with a promotional logo. He got it free. 'I thought, it's not a bad shirt, and the bloke gave it to me,' he explains.

Another new economy interviewee stresses the importance of

reliability in business. 'Reliability is part of a good work ethic,' he states emphatically.

In my interview with Donald Carey (an assumed name), the echoes of Weber are especially strong. Carey emphasises the work ethic and thrift throughout the interview. 'I mean, I've had my nose to the grindstone for about 100 years,' he declares. 'I'm interested in achievement. It doesn't mean that I don't have hobbies or other interesting things. I probably spend a great deal of time working — more than most people do. I don't back off at four o'clock and go to a pub. I barely drink ... I can take it or leave it. I don't smoke.

'There's a very interesting book called *The Millionaire Next Door*. If you haven't read it, you ought to get a copy. It'll cost you $18.95.'

As it happens, I have read *The Millionaire Next Door*. The book is an American bestseller based on a survey of American millionaires. Its main point is that wealth is not about luck or inheritance or education or intelligence. In the words of the authors: 'Wealth is more often the result of a lifestyle of hard work, perseverence, planning, and, most of all, self-discipline.' The spirit of capitalism, more or less. I am struck by the fact that Carey tells me its price is $18.95. Not 'about $20', which is what I would say — $18.95 exactly.

At another point in the interview Carey talks about what is required to make a successful business. 'You've got to put your head down and your backside up and work, I'd say, probably 70 or 80 hours a week for quite a long time, and have the good Lord with you as well.

'So I believe in the white Anglo-Saxon Protestant work ethic, and I'm a living example of it.'

Carey returns repeatedly to the theme of thrift. For example, he talks about how *The Millionaire Next Door* shows that 'the one thing that all millionaires have in common is that they are thrifty, thrifty,

thrifty'. And the main ethnic origin of these millionaires? 'Guess what — Scots!' He acknowledges his own Scottish ancestry. 'That's where I get my meanness from!' he says matter-of-factly.

A moment later I describe an Australian study about the ethnic origins of wealth in earlier times. He anticipates the findings of the study before I complete my sentence.

'White Anglo-Saxon Protestant!' he declares.

Donald Carey frames his values in terms of the Protestant work ethic. Yet he has nothing to say about religion. When I ask him about religion, he shifts the conversation to religious values. 'I grew up as a white Anglo-Saxon Protestant,' he says. 'I believe in those values and I practise what I preach.' He then elaborates on commercial honesty and reliability, emphasising their economic advantages.

'I believe that if you've got a customer [with a problem] you fix it, no matter what it costs you, because then you've got a friend. The other way you've got a mortal enemy for life.'

Carey is typical of the people I interview in his lack of religious attachment. None of the entrepreneurs I meet declare strong religious convictions; many are antagonistic.

When I ask Clive Berghofer about religion, for example, he says he has probably never been in a church in his life. His mother was reared as a very strict Catholic, but 'she went away from it, because she could see how bigoted they could be'.

'They're selling fuckin' blue sky, mate,' says another man. 'It's like Communism!'

A third man says that religion is 'such a restrictive thought process that it's an actual hindrance'.

Among the super rich, hard work, thrift, sobriety and so on are overwhelmingly secular values.

In the early 1980s the Australian sociologist Jane Marceau studied the owners of small manufacturing enterprises and their values. Many of these owners had fathers who operated small businesses — like the super rich. Many were themselves 'not very far from the working class'. Like Clive Berghofer, they came up through manual work and trades occupations to their present position.

> 'YOU NEED TO BE OBSESSED. YOU NEED TO BE FANATICAL.'

Marceau went on to distinguish between 'livelihood entrepreneurs' and 'growth entrepreneurs'. The overwhelming majority of the owners in her study were livelihood entrepreneurs, individuals who wanted a livelihood from their business. They valued being their own boss, controlling their own lives and making their own decisions. They were not much worried about growing the business. Only a tiny minority (4 per cent) of the owners in the study were growth entrepreneurs. These individuals wanted more than a livelihood. They wanted an empire.

The super rich, of course, are mostly growth entrepreneurs. The people I interview took their businesses from one level to the next, then to the next. Their commitment goes beyond the work ethic.

'It's not necessarily the money that drives you,' says Gerry Harvey. 'It's just that you're driven.'

'You need to be obsessed,' says Brett Blundy. 'You need to be fanatical.' He adds that it's the only way to do what he's done.

'I think you have to be really single-minded and driven,' another interviewee emphasises. 'In the end, you can't *decide* to be that way. And if you are that way, it's pretty hard to stop.'

A measure of the growth orientation of these people is how the business subsumes their families. Entrepreneurs consistently describe how the growth of their businesses depended upon intense family cooperation, especially 'accommodating' wives. Alternatively, they describe marital breakdown, and sometimes the neglect of their children. One interviewee's choice of words is revealing.

'As everyone would tell you,' he says, 'you have to be totally single-minded. You just have to be. Basically what you do is — you do business and you have family.'

You *do* business. You *have* family.

'I don't know of anyone who has made a fist of anything like my business who hasn't devoted themself to it entirely,' he adds. 'It just doesn't happen.'

Another measure of the growth orientation of the super rich is how disinclined they are towards retirement. Take, for example, Harry Tyrrell, who built up a manufacturing business in the 1950s and 1960s and is now in his eighties. He says he used to work seven days a week, twelve hours a day, for years. 'Your wife has to be 100 per cent behind you, and put up with all the inconvenience and so on,' he emphasises. 'When I retired from the company ten years or so ago, I went home that night and I said to my wife, "Oh well, I'll see you in the morning — I'll be going to work."' He smiles. 'I still come to work on a Saturday.'

I'm not surprised. When I first tried to arrange an interview, Tyrrell suggested the upcoming public holiday. I declined with embarrassment — I had already made plans to take the long weekend off.

As it happens, one interviewee — Bill James, a big stakeholder in the travel retailer Flight Centre — does not describe himself as driven, obsessed or single-minded. He retired in 1997, after Flight Centre became a public company. When I interview him, he has just returned home from a round of golf. He is philosophical and self-deprecating.

James describes himself as coming from 'a very, very average — average being the operative word — upbringing'.

'There's nothing in my family that would lend itself to say that it prepared me for the world of business,' he says emphatically. His father worked for a builder. 'He was their leading hand, their carpenter and did a lot of the ordering.' He was 'a bright guy', but 'the antithesis of a businessman'. James's mother was a housewife who thought school teaching was 'the top of the pile'. Her ambitions for her son extended to his becoming a teacher.

James went to the local Catholic school and did well enough to get into university, where he studied economics. Following university he taught for a year and hated it. Then in 1973 he headed off on a working holiday. He landed in 'Bazza McKenzie's London', where he met Graham Turner — or 'Screw' as he was known, on account of his surname. Turner was another young Australian on a working holiday.

'Met at a party,' James explains. 'One thing led to another. He bought a double-decker bus, I was passenger number one and we went to Morocco. The business started like that.'

James jumps ahead in his story. 'I guess the reason why I stuck at that ... was that he was the visionary. He was the guy with the ideas. I would never have done what I've done if I hadn't met him. You know what I mean? I just sort of tagged along and went along for the ride, hanging on to his shirt tail.'

Before their departure for Morocco, Turner placed an advertisement in the *Australasian Express* for a second double-decker bus tour. 'When we got back,' James recalls, 'seventeen people had rung up to book and pay for the second trip. I thought, shit, we've got a business on our hands!'

James invested his savings in a second bus. Thereafter they kept advertising for more customers, and running more trips, and buying more buses. The business, called Top Deck, went from strength to strength. 'We ended up with with 100 buses over nine, ten years,' James remarks. 'So it just boomed.'

In 1983, though, the business almost collapsed. 'We were insolvent,' James says, 'absolutely and utterly insolvent.' He recalls his words to Turner on the phone. 'It's all over, mate,' he had said. 'We're overdrawn by 80 000 quid. The banks are about to knock back the cheques. We're stuffed!'

But Turner was not finished yet. He divisionalised the business, making the profit and loss centres more transparent. In the process he turned the venture from a London-based tour operator into an Australia-based discount travel retailer — Flight Centre. The business survived and thrived. In 1995 it became a public company, catapulting its major shareholders into the limelight and the Rich Lists.

James cannot emphasise Turner's influence enough. Turner built the business, Turner made the money. James describes Turner as the 'most out-of-the-square thinker I've ever met'. He talks about his personal tenacity, drive and ambition. 'This guy knows no bounds in terms of what can or cannot be achieved,' he reflects. 'He has been an unbelievable role model for me. That's the source of all of my wealth, in the sense that I was smart enough to recognise that this guy was absolutely unique and, if I hung around him, I'd be wealthy. I knew that from the day I met him in London in '73, and it has proved to be correct.'

When James decided to retire from Flight Centre, he reviewed his priorities. 'Two years after the float [of the company] I thought, what's life all about? — I don't need the business as the means of a purpose in my life.' His current priority is to enjoy life and be with his family. He also indulges his interest in the big questions, such as quantum physics, and 'thinking about the spiritual world, like philosophy and that sort of stuff'. There is a downside though: he gets less social recognition, and doesn't meet people now 'like Screw meets people as chief executive officer'.

'But the advantage is, I can wake up in the morning and do what I bloody well want to do. Yesterday I played golf, today I played golf, I'm talking with you now. I'm the chief cook and bottle washer. I do a lot of domestic chores around the house and run the kids here, there and everywhere. So basically I enjoy life and try to spend more time with my family.'

Some people who amass great fortunes are not driven, obsessed and single-minded. But they attach themselves to people with these qualities. In James' disarming words, they 'hang on to their shirt tails'. And then they retire. They are the exceptions who prove the rule.

Several months after the interview, Bill James sends me a copy of his just-published book *Top Deck Daze*, the story of Top Deck and the origins of Flight Centre. The book is a tribute to Turner and describes the precise moment at which James decided to attach himself to Turner's shirt tail.

Turner and his friend Geoff ('Spy') Lomas had bought their double-decker bus, and assembled fourteen Australian and New Zealand backpackers for a jaunt to Morocco. The bus had made its way to the Spanish port of Algeciras, where it was to go by ferry across the Strait of Gibraltar. At the docks a ticket clerk told them that their double-decker bus was too big for the ferry — that it wouldn't fit in. At the tourist office they found out that no other ferries

> 'WE WERE ALWAYS ENTREPRENEURIAL AND OPPORTUNISTIC. WE WERE NEVER PREPARED JUST TO ACCEPT THE STATUS QUO.'

in Spain were servicing the route at that time of year. They then tried all of the shipping agents in town, without success.

At this point Turner, Lomas and James settled into a bar by the docks and drank in silence while the ferry came and went. James suggested more time in Spain. Turner dismissed the idea. James suggested driving on to Portugal. Turner ignored him. 'The more we drank,' James recalled, 'the more I abused Screw for his pigheadedness and inability to accept the facts. We couldn't get to Morocco, and that was that. The more I appealed to him to see reason, the more he refused to talk with me.'

After a long and unpleasant lunch, Turner rose abruptly. He instructed Lomas to get the passengers on the bus and park it close by, out of sight from the docks. Lomas and James followed instructions. Then, five minutes before the departure of the last ferry of the day, 'Screw came running towards us, jumped into the driver's cab, fired up the engine and hurtled the bus through the terminal gates, only slowing enough to throw a ferry ticket at the gatekeeper through the open window of the cab'. They drove furiously around the terminal building, catching sight of the last car passing through the ferry door. *Top Deck Daze* continues:

> Screw ignored the frantic gesticulating of the stevedores as they jumped clear of the bus as it careered up the narrow ramp. There was a horrible grinding noise as the chassis scraped the lip of the stern as we came level with the deck. There was just enough room for the bus to perch on the ferry's rear deck, with the bus's top deck inches from the ferry door, and its back platform overhanging the ferry's stern so far that if you stepped off, you'd go straight into the Mediterranean Sea.

Before they knew it, they were on their way to Morocco.

The incident had a profound effect on James. Turner had refused to acknowledge defeat, he'd broken the rules and he'd got the bus onto the ferry. James, on the other hand, had 'willingly accepted defeat'. The event had highlighted his 'conservatism and narrowness of thought'. James decided that if the opportunity arose he would 'work with or near Screw in any capacity possible'. The opportunity did arise, and James made a fortune.

The incident reflects common themes in my interviews. The entrepreneurs I meet are an unusual bunch of people. Their business histories consistently involve breaking rules, taking risks and seizing opportunities. Occasionally interviewees reflect in general terms on these qualities. One man, for example, tries to explain his family's passage from one enterprise to another. 'We were always entrepreneurial and opportunistic,' he says. 'We were never prepared just to accept the status quo.'

Another reflects, 'Entrepreneurs are by definition — the ones I've come across — extremely individualistic people. It's a sort of character trait, whereas other people are more comfortable forming themselves into a group.'

More commonly, these themes come out in the stories. As the interviews progress, I am struck by how often the people thread their stories together by reference to opportunity. The interviewees are always alert to opportunity. It is the thread that links one business enterprise with the next. In turn, it drives the entrepreneurial narrative.

'We're reasonably diversified, and yet one business sort of built off the other,' says one man at the very beginning of the interview. 'There was never any plan — it was just the way opportunities came along ... We just saw an opportunity, and went with it and developed it.'

A moment later he remarks, 'Then an opportunity came along.'

He uses this or a similar phrase again and again throughout the conversation.

Interviewees talk about opportunity reflexively, so I press them further, asking them to reflect on their motivation. At this point they often struggle for words, but eventually they arrive at terms such as 'achievement' and 'challenge'. Consider, for example, Jim Ward (not his real name), who took over his father's business and grew it dramatically. His father, he says, was mainly concerned 'about survival' — in Marceau's terms, a livelihood entrepreneur.

I ask about his own motivation for expanding the business.

'I saw that question [on the list],' Ward says carefully. 'Well, I think it was ego as much as anything else, or the desire to be seen to succeed.' He adds that he 'only ever wanted to be the best' in his line of business.

Damien Cook (an assumed name) struggles to explain his motivation. I ask what made him expand his business beyond a means to a livelihood.

'I don't know,' he says.

'You don't know?'

'I *do* know,' he replies. 'I remember hitting that wall when I bought [another business] — no, just before. I was in negotiations, and they were very tough. I remember this very vividly. It's an interesting question ...

'That was the first time that I'd been in a very heavy negotiation, and I thought, oh God, this is all too hard! I was earning $150 000 a year — that was back in the mid-seventies — and I thought, gee, that's not a bad income and it will probably grow to $250 000 and that's a quarter of a million dollars a year. That's more than I can possibly spend, so why do it?

'And I've come up against that two or three times since — that feeling of, "Look, isn't this enough?" But then I feel, "Hang on, you're going soft. Can't you cope with a challenge — what's wrong with you? Why don't you stiffen up and push through?"

'And each time, I've stiffened up and pushed through.'

There is a contradiction here. Entrepreneurs such as Damien Cook have an enormous sense of agency. They seize opportunities, they drive through obstacles, they build business empires. Yet there is still an inner voice that goads Cook on to the next challenge: 'Can't you cope? What's wrong with you?' My guess is that growth entrepreneurs commonly experience an inner voice of this sort. It comes from the past — the Holocaust, a father's death, bankruptcy, childhood insecurity, whatever. This is why entrepreneurs describe themselves as 'driven', in the passive form of the verb. Someone else — something else — is in the driver's seat. They themselves are on one hell of a ride.

Chapter Five

Dynasty

Secrets of the super rich

'I DO NOT WANT THIS INTERVIEW RECORDED!'

Harold Jackson — as I will call him — is a patriarch of the old school. He has a reputation for carefully guarded privacy and I was amazed when he agreed to talk with me. On the appointed day he greets me enthusiastically. 'I've been so looking forward to this,' he says, pumping my hand.

We make our way to a meeting room. I begin to take my cassette recorder from my briefcase. His mood shifts abruptly. 'I do not want this interview recorded!' he says firmly. I try to explain the reasons for recording the interview. While I am usually persuasive in these circumstances, Jackson is unmoved. I try again, but he is still unmoved. I can see that nothing I say will change his mind and I resign myself to taking notes.

Throughout the interview Jackson is torn between three cross-cutting impulses. First, he is proud of his achievements and happy to speak of them. He has built a mighty company, working alongside his brothers. At times the interview rolls along mightily, as I frenetically scribble notes. Second, Jackson is deeply troubled by family and succession issues and wants to talk through these matters. He runs the business with an iron fist but doesn't control the shareholding. A growing number of family shareholders are demanding more of a say in the business. Our conversation seems invariably to thread its way back to the topic of family and succession. Finally, and notwithstanding this, Jackson is intensely private and is especially fearful about any public airing of family brawls over succession. In talking about the family fortune he opens up on the subject, but then reflexively closes down again. The interview repeatedly grinds to a halt.

As usual, the first question I ask is about the Rich Lists. His view is predictable: they are very embarrassing, they offend his concern for privacy. 'When they first came out, we approached a lawyer to find out whether we had any right of appeal against this kind of action, and whether we could take them to court. We were advised that we had no right of appeal.

'It's very intrusive to have your name appear in public like that. If you go to the club or the golf club, you're just one of the boys; you're not someone who has a huge fortune.'

Jackson then launches into the history of his family business. He is on a roll, talking about the 'Puritan' ethic of the family and its emphasis on hard work. And like others before him, he talks about opportunity. 'We've just taken advantage of opportunities as we see them,' he says. 'These opportunities occur. If you can identify them and hop in and take advantage, then you're set. Private companies seem to be able to take advantage more quickly than public companies in these situations.'

The subject of wealth accumulation reminds Jackson of why he has agreed to this interview in the first place. He refers me back to the letter I sent him. 'I am intrigued by your approach in this study — the fact that you're starting off with the *Business Review Weekly* Rich Lists, and you're looking at the wealth that has been created and then looking at the issue of family.

'My wife tells me that I am too focused on the business and not enough on the family. I've been battered with this "family approach" in the past few years.'

Jackson describes himself as an autocrat. But he also acknowledges growing pressure from family shareholders — brothers, sons and daughters, nephews and nieces, and all of their spouses. Some of them are pushing for a family approach. They want a more transparent and democratic business structure for the shareholders — such things as family meetings, family councils and 'family constitutions'. They point to the application of such an approach in the United States and within some family businesses in Australia.

Jackson is not impressed. He thinks that the family approach is nonsense; that the shareholders who advocate it are talkers, not doers. They don't understand the requirements of a successful business. 'In the past,' he explains, 'we ignored the shareholders. We ploughed the dividends back into the business. We paid practically nothing in the way of dividends.

'The dividends *have* been increasing lately,' he adds. 'We still don't pay a lot of dividends, but we're providing more information. But the more the shareholders are told, the more dissatisfied they become.'

Yet Jackson is finding it increasingly difficult to hold back the pressure for reform. This is at least partly because he has already diluted his own shareholding in the business. He passed on his wealth in the 1970s, before the abolition of death duties. 'I was worried about the effects of death duties,' he explains, 'and so I distributed my estate in a way that was going to minimise those death duties.'

He gave two-thirds of his estate to the 'boys' and one-third to the 'girls', which he says was probably considered normal then. The idea was that the sons would join the family business. Favouring his sons improved the chances of a family business dynasty surviving across generations. This was because the family shareholding remained concentrated in fewer hands. It also kept down the numbers of shareholders who were not in the business.

'Nowadays things have changed,' Jackson reflects. 'There's more of a view that boys and girls should receive the assets equally. In the 1970s it was in more of a transitional phase.'

The shareholding has now become more complicated, with the family shareholders increasingly polarised. Jackson is puzzled, hurt and defiant. He believes that if he gives way to the family rebels, the business will suffer and everyone will be worse off.

Towards the end of the interview I ask him for his views on the debate about an Australian republic. It causes him to reflect again on dynastic succession in families.

'It is so unfortunate that we have to pay lip service to someone like Prince Charles,' he replies. 'We can simply do better than that. You get this sort of thing in all families — the weak and the strong.'

Jackson is in no doubt about who are the weak and who are the strong in his own family. But he is finding it increasingly difficult to hold back the growing numbers of the weak and keep the conflict contained in the privacy of his family empire. He is determined to hold the fort for as long as he is able.

Liz Turner — an assumed name — has rebelled against her family. She describes herself as 'an inveterate people-pleaser almost all of my life'. In her family she was 'the devoted daughter — devoted, trusting and naive'. The experience of challenging her family has been overwhelmingly traumatic. 'I almost needed a full-frontal lobotomy!' she says. 'I needed a real head change, or mind shift.'

> 'I THINK THAT IF YOU LIVE BY THE SWORD, YOU DIE BY THE SWORD.'

Turner's parents came from a working-class background. Her father, she says, was tremendously driven and had a huge capacity for work. Her mother was fiercely ambitious, and determined that she would provide opportunities for her own children.

The relationship, Turner explains, was very much a partnership. 'It wasn't the way society viewed it. How it appeared was that Dad was the driver of the expansion and development of the company, while Mum had been allocated the domestic and childrearing tasks. But she did a lot more than that behind the scenes.' Even so, the division of labour between Turner's parents in the home was conventional. Her father worked long hours at the business; her mother looked after the children. Turner recalls how her mother explained her father's unavailability. '"Your father is a fantastic father," she would say, "because he is making this huge sacrifice for you children, in order to secure your future."'

From his early years, Turner's parents groomed their only son for the family business. They did not do the same for their daughters. Turner strives to recall any suggestion that she might have a future in the business. 'It was never offered,' she says. 'It was never mentioned. It was never even joked about. There was nothing that ever hinted at any possibility that I would ever be part of the management structure.' On the other hand, she has no difficulty in recalling the pressure to get married and have children. 'The general feeling was that if I didn't get married,' she says, 'I would be a miserable old spinster.'

She remembers getting lectures from her parents about how she was too independent. Finally she married and had children, while her brother forged a career in the family business.

Turner describes her main role in life as that of the dutiful daughter. She started questioning this role when her brother approached her about selling her stake in the family trust. Turner asked for clarification. 'The more I started delving,' she comments, 'the more nervous he became and the more irritated he became with my attitude. How dare I ask questions!' She eventually discovered that her father had already narrowed the ownership of the family business, favouring his son over the daughters.

She recalls her distress: 'I said, "Dad, you've just deprived me of a voice! You've just given away my inheritance! Why did no one tell me? Is this the reason why nobody wanted to give me any documents?"

'He said, "They're worth nothing anyway. You've always trusted us to look after you. Your brother will look after you. There's no reason for you to have those voting units."'

This discovery led to a breakdown in family relationships. Turner says she felt betrayed and abandoned. It also crystallised her growing unease about succession in the family business. Her brother's children were following in the footsteps of their father: they were part of the 'inner sanctum' of the business and had 'wondrous opportunities to see the world and gain corporate experience'. Her own children — and those of her sister — were on the outer.

Turner was terrified of challenging her family. She refers repeatedly to the 'obsessive need for privacy' in the family. She knew that if she did rebel, there would be a closing of the ranks. 'I knew that with the family you're either in or out. There are no shades of grey. I was either the darling daughter and treasured sister, or I was Public Enemy Number One.'

She explains how she overcame her terror. 'I think what empowered me was the pain — the huge, overwhelming, almost life-threatening pain that I felt in what I saw as rejection, abandonment, betrayal, but predominantly the invalidation of my whole life.

'I felt that I was a really loving, caring, intelligent, contributing member of the family in so many ways. I played the role that I believed was expected of me, and I did it gladly and lovingly. I felt that I had been repaid with brutality.'

The brutality left her with an overwhelming feeling of emptiness. She felt that she had nothing left to lose.

Turner is now locked in harsh combat. She recalls one of the meetings with her brother: 'At the end of the meeting my brother said, "We have nothing to discuss, unless you agree with me."

'I said, "But that's not negotiation!"

'He said, "Well, that's it. I'm not interested in giving you anything. There's nothing in it for me." Then he said, "If you want to take this further, take us to court! You've got no case." He told me several times to take it to court. When I did, he was absolutely incensed.

'I just think it's really baffling and irksome for him that this little person is not going to be squashed. There are a lot more issues at stake here, apart from the money. I feel that it's more about control than anything. He wants to be in control of the family.'

Turner is trying to put enough pressure on her father and brother to bring them to the negotiating table. 'My office here is almost full of files that I study on a daily basis,' she says. 'It really is a full-time job for me. It's a commitment I've made.' She adds that she has information that the family would not want placed in the public domain. She will use it if she has no choice.

'I think that if you live by the sword, you die by the sword,' she says defiantly.

Each entrepreneur I interview has his or her own story of making a fortune. Each story is different in its details, yet every story is the same in its structure — an account of triumph over adversity. It evokes the fairy tales and myths from our childhood. *Once upon a time there was a young man or woman of humble circumstances. They set off on a long journey, facing many tests and trials along the way. Finally they achieve a great fortune.*

The people I interview tell their stories with the confidence that arises from that triumph over adversity. Occasionally the fairy tale pops out of the narrative. One interviewee describes how the dream of a 'pot of gold' came true on the listing of his business. Another man describes the pleasure of 'sitting on a pile of money' beyond his wildest imagination.

Young entrepreneurs know no other narrative. They are flushed with success. They are brimming with confidence. They see only new challenges on the horizon. One man, for example, explains that he is not concerned about passing on his estate. 'I think you do all this for the challenge, the fun of doing it,' he says enthusiastically. 'You don't do it because you want to get a gold-lined casket or coffin, you know.' Another man describes his attitude towards the global economy. 'It scares me not at all. All it does is keep throwing up opportunities, from our point of view — which is great. It's great! I love it!'

Among older entrepreneurs, another story follows the first. It is the story of succession — what happens to the business empire and the money in the long run. Ultimately it is about what will happen beyond the lifetime of the founder. This story is no longer a triumphal story. The people I interview become more uncertain at this point. The course of the narrative becomes more uncertain; the outcomes become more uncertain. Everyone does not live happily ever after.

The story of *making* a fortune is mostly the story of individuals. There are one or two key individuals who build the empire. They are almost always men. The family may be important, but there are usually

> **'I DON'T KNOW WHY I'M TELLING YOU THESE THINGS.'**

one or two family members who provide the leadership. As Bill James might put it, the family hangs on to the shirt tails of these people.

In the story of *passing* on a fortune, the family — not least the women — becomes much more important. Sons and daughters, nephews and nieces, grandchildren and great grandchildren move to the centre of the narrative. I interview some of this larger cast of characters — including Liz Turner. Their story is not a triumphal one either. These people have many stories to tell — such as walking in the footsteps of the father, the weight of great expectations, and the breakup of family relationships.

When entrepreneurs talk about wealth accumulation, they talk overwhelmingly about themselves. As they consider family business succession, their gaze turns outwards. Interviewees talk about other families. In particular, they regularly reflect on the big dynastic fortunes — the Murdochs, the Packers, the Lowys, and the Pratts. They also talk about the Smorgon family, which was once a shining example of family business succession and which has now divided its assets among different branches of the family. One man, for example, reflects on the future of his own family business. 'Ultimately it could be best to sell the bloody lot,' he suggests, 'and let everybody do . . . what all the Smorgons are doing at the moment.'

Interviewees struggle with conflicting impulses in telling their own story of succession. On the one hand, people want to talk. There is a huge fortune at stake. There is a cast of characters with a stake in the fortune. There are deep emotions at work. In some instances there are vicious family conflicts. Sometimes people tell the story almost in spite of themselves: the story — or bits and pieces of it — bursts out of them. Harold Jackson keeps returning to the subjects of family and succession in spite of himself. Another man says quizzically, 'I don't know why I'm telling you these things.'

On the other hand, there is a code of secrecy within families concerning succession. Families present a united front to the world. Liz Turner talks about the 'family dogma of the inner sanctum'. The high stakes maintain the code of secrecy: the people I interview are concerned about causing business damage and family damage. They become *especially* concerned about anonymity on the subject of succession. They phone me after the interview to warn that certain comments should be suppressed. They become tight-lipped. Occasionally the silences are deafening.

Family members break the code of secrecy when they believe that they have nothing left to lose. Liz Turner is at that point. She refers to the 'obsessive need for privacy' in her family. 'I knew that with the family you're either in or out,' she says. The desire for secrecy is itself a bargaining chip as she tries to bring her family to the negotiating table.

'SUCCESSION IS EVERYTHING!'

The celebrated American economist Oliver Williamson explained the enduring importance of family business in Western economies in two words: 'cheap labour'. He could have added 'cheap money'. This explanation is — typically — grounded in rational self-interest. It contains some truth, especially in relation to the start-up phase of the business. Many interviewees emphasise that family members worked long hours for small personal rewards, putting profits back into the business.

'We ploughed the dividends back into the business,' Harold Jackson recalls. 'We paid practically nothing in the way of dividends.'

'We didn't even take home the basic wage for many years,' says another man. 'We kept the money in the company and just built it, and built it, and built it.'

At the same time, cheap labour (and money) is not the whole story. There is another word — 'trust' — that also goes a long way in explaining the enduring importance of family business in Western economies. The noted American sociologist Francis Fukuyama observed in his book entitled *Trust* that the model of the self-interested individual overlooks the role of trust. The greatest economic efficiency, he argued, is 'not necessarily achieved by rational self-interested individuals but rather by groups of individuals who, because of a pre-existing moral community, are able to work together effectively.'

Trust is the reason that family members work long hours for small personal rewards, ploughing profits back into the business. They are confident that their sacrifice will be repaid. In turn, entrepreneurs trust family members to work hard and long for the business. They have a stake in its future.

'By management, for management!' one interviewee says dismissively. 'That's why I want my kids to come in, because I don't have a high opinion of professional management.'

Trust and cheap labour explain family business up to a point, especially among small and medium-size businesses. But only up to a point. They do not explain family business on the largest scale, where the business already has a large professional workforce. After all, the largest Australian fortunes are dynastic, with fathers grooming their sons — not just as owners but as executive managers. There are the media empires of Rupert Murdoch and Kerry Packer, there is the shopping mall empire of Frank Lowy, there is the paper manufacturing empire of Richard Pratt. Family business on the largest scale arises from the ambition to forge a dynasty. The patriarchs and matriarchs are looking beyond their own lifetimes. They want their children to carry on their work — to extend the empire across generations. For their part, it is difficult for the children to turn their backs on the opportunity. The family business is a glittering prize, offering wealth, status and power.

The people I interview are often reluctant to acknowledge a dynastic ambition. Yet the ambition is frequently implicit in their actions and simmers beneath the surface of the interview. Above all, the super rich groom their sons, and occasionally their daughters, to take over the management of the business. One man, for example, recalls that his father said to him, 'You're the trustee of this business.' In turn, the business would mean nothing to this man without the involvement of his own children. 'Family succession in terms of the business means something,' he emphasises. 'In terms of assets, it doesn't mean anything. Succession is everything!'

The dynastic ambition is especially apparent when it is thwarted. Rod Myer's biography of the industrialist Victor Smorgon, *Living the Dream: The Story of Victor Smorgon*, describes how Smorgon experienced an ebbing of his life purpose following the sale of the family empire: 'Without the family working together his life had little meaning. The success was something he was thankful for but in some ways he felt like a failure. His dream had been to create a dynasty like the Rothschilds that would last 200 years or more and that dream was shattered.'

Smorgon promptly used his money from the sale of the business to start building another business empire, the Victor Smorgon Group, with his grandson. He 'still harbours his dream of the long-surviving dynasty'.

Similarly, David Langer (not his real name) wanted his sons to join his business, but they didn't share his ambition — they had their own. Langer lurches between different emotions as he describes their decision not to follow him in the business. First he is resigned, as befits an interview in the public domain. 'They have always been very polite,' he says. Then there is a flash of anger as he complains that it was 'below their dignity to come into their father's business'. Collecting himself, he reflects that not many children go into their parents' business. 'There are the Lowys who went in,' he remarks. 'The Pratts — sort of. Who else? Not many.'

Next he pays tribute to his sons. He also provides an explanation for their decision, almost in spite of himself. 'They're intelligent boys,' he says. 'They saw me working from early in the morning to late at night and nothing else.' Then he relives the way he lost his temper with one son over his refusal to join the business and didn't speak with his son for a long time. 'But in the long run,' he adds, 'I gave in. I've got no choice. He's still my son.'

Later in the interview Langer returns to the subject. It haunts him. Beneath the anger, there is grief. He finds it hard to acknowledge the grief. 'I wasn't successful — no,' Langer says. 'Disappointed, probably, yes. Many times I lie in bed and try to read a book, but...' His voice trails off, and then he picks himself up. 'Yes, disappointed. My children know that, but they look at it differently.'

> **'I THINK IT DEPENDS ENTIRELY ON HOW MANY IDIOTS YOU BREED.'**

The dream of a dynasty is powerful, but it is also deeply ambivalent. For a start, the individuals who accumulated the fortune are often too driven to find the time to prepare their children to take over the job, and too driven to stand aside for the children. It is too much like getting ready to die. In any case, their children are not usually driven in the same way as themselves — they grew up in very different circumstances. Patriarchs distrust their children's commitment and ability to manage the business. What if they blow away the work of a lifetime?

Take, for example, Donald Carey — which, as I've said, is an assumed name. Carey prides himself on his hard work and his 'meanness', which laid the groundwork for his fortune. I ask him whether keeping the business in the family is an important consideration.

'Well,' he says matter-of-factly, 'I think it depends entirely on how many idiots you breed.'

Carey still works like a man possessed, doubting that his sons are capable of taking over the reins even if they want to. 'I'm bound to say that is a bit of a disappointment to me,' he says. 'However it comes back to what I said: when it comes to children, you get what you are given.' Carey is pinning his dynastic hopes on his grandsons. In the meantime he depends upon professional managers.

It is not just the individuals who accumulated the fortune who experience deep ambivalence. Their children are also ambivalent. The family business is a glittering prize, but it carries a cost. The children must first serve their time, working in the long shadow of their parents. How long before the prize comes into their own hands? How long before they are able to make their own mark on the world? How long before they can emerge from the shadow of their parents?

In some circumstances, the family business becomes a psychological prison for the children. One interviewee, for example, recalls that he joined the business automatically. He could not conceive of a life outside it because, he says, he was 'really unemployable elsewhere'. But he was intensely unhappy in the business. The upshot was 'the beginnings of psychotic depression triggered by a feeling of helplessness'. He was, he says straightforwardly, a prisoner of the system.

A notorious court case *Moran v. Moran* — played out before the New South Wales Supreme Court in early 2000 highlights the way in which a family business can become a psychological prison. Murray Waldren has told the story of this court case in his book *Moran v. Moran*. The person at the centre of the case was Doug Moran, who had accumulated a fortune through nursing homes. In 2000 the *BRW* Rich List estimated that he was worth $300 million, the sixty-third richest man in Australia. The estimate was probably conservative.

Moran grew up in dire poverty. He ran away from home at the age of thirteen and became a cabin boy on a ship. In his twenties he went into developing real estate. In his thirties he moved into developing nursing homes, with the support of his wife Greta. When Moran featured in the inaugural 1983 Rich List, he wrote to congratulate *BRW* for 'giving public recognition to some of Australia's achievers'. He was proud of his achievement.

The Morans had seven children. All of them joined the family business at some stage, which provided them with generous salary packages, company cars, expense accounts (including clothing) and big loan accounts.

In mid-1994 the Morans' sixth-born child, Brendan, left the business. Following his resignation Doug and Greta disowned him, cutting off all support. They also pursued him for the repayment of a $250 000 home loan, which Brendan had understood was a gift. In an undated letter Doug warned him: 'Anything that happens from this date on is now on your own head. No family member will be in sympathy with the results that you cause to yourself and your family. Should they not concur, they too will suffer in a similar manner.'

Note here the threat against the other children. It certainly seemed as if Doug ruled the family with an iron fist: the children were either in or out; there was nothing in between. Several months later Doug and Greta, in an interview with *Business Review Weekly*, talked about business, family and succession planning. A family photograph of the couple surrounded by six of their seven children left no doubt that Brendan was out of the picture in every sense.

Kristina Moran, Brendan's wife at the time, reported that following publication a big yellow envelope containing a copy of the magazine was left at Brendan's front door. Someone had written on the envelope: 'Notice you didn't get a mention. Loser!' Parts of the article itself had been highlighted. Brendan assumed that the package had been left by his older brother Peter. His wife Kristina recalled in court that Brendan was really annoyed. 'He threw it down and said, "Thanks Peter." Just threw it on the floor; he was really, really upset.'

Brendan could not cope with life outside the family, and quickly unravelled. He tried a job in real estate but couldn't keep it. His marriage disintegrated. In early 1995 he considered his position in note form, under the heading 'What are my options?'. The first option was 'Kill myself', which was accompanied by three ticks. The second option was 'Sort out this mess! How?' This was followed by the names of possible employers. He also considered variations of this course of action; that is, 'Write a book' and 'Change my name'. The final option was to contact a motivational coach. This option was negated immediately by 'Cannot afford'. At the end of the list Brendan wrote: 'How? Carbon monoxide poisoning!!!!'

Two days later Brendan gassed himself in a rented car. The process took about 90 minutes. As he inhaled the fumes, he scrawled a ten-page chronicle, raging against his family. For example: 'I rejoice in the fact that I by leaving this world will never have to put up with any of that crap that has been given to me continually through my life. The bashings, beatings and humiliations, publicly and privately, have become so great that I have nothing to live for.'

In his final minutes, Brendan circled his comment: 'I'm not scared, my parents don't rip me off in death.'

Brendan could not conceive of a realistic course of action other than taking his own life. After the suicide, Doug and Greta continued to pursue Brendan's widow Kristina for repayment of the home loan. In response, Kristina sued the Morans for 'mental shock'. The subsequent court case included allegations that Doug had regularly beaten Greta, and had engaged in humiliating extramarital affairs; that Greta had undergone a course of electroshock therapy as treatment for depression; and that the first-born son Peter had seriously bullied Brendan at work, including hanging him up by his own tie in the company car park, and biting his finger to the bone.

> 'YOU'RE STUCK ON IT. YOU ALL HAVE TO WORK THERE AND WAIT UNTIL DAD DIES OR SOMETHING.'

Doug Moran finally settled the case just before he was to give evidence, but the damage was already done. The family secrecy was blown to smithereens. So was its reputation. Brendan had taken his revenge.

Several months before *Moran v. Moran* comes to court, I interview Kerry Jones, the Morans' first-born child. She's friendly, but tight-lipped on the subject of family business dynamics. She says nothing to suggest family divisions and conflicts. I have several interviews like this — where the silences are louder than anything that is said. In these instances, family secrets keep the interviews on an unshakeably superficial track.

By the same token, some interviewees go down another track. They leave no doubt that there are many points of division and conflict around the question of bringing the offspring into the family business. Liz Turner is a case in point, as we have seen. Her father trained his son to manage the family business; he did not train either of his daughters. Now he has taken a step further. He has arranged his succession planning so that his son will inherit the bulk of the estate. This course of action follows a longstanding patriarchal tradition designed to guarantee a family dynasty. It prevents the dispersal of the family estate.

The longer the dynastic succession, the more complex the family business becomes — as in the case of Harold Jackson. Brothers, sisters and cousins work alongside each other. They also work alongside the husbands and wives of their brothers, sisters and cousins. Some family members join the business, whereas others do not. Professional managers join the business, working alongside family management. The more complex the family business, the more scope there is for division and conflict — hence the multiple lines of conflict in Harold Jackson's empire.

Division and conflict arise because family members are more differentiated. They no longer share a common upbringing. They are attached to the business in different ways. In turn, it is more difficult to maintain trust. There are tensions between different branches of the family. And there are tensions between family members who work in the business and family members who have shares in the business.

One interviewee, James Armstrong (as I'll call him), describes these multi-generation family businesses as 'tight structures'. He speaks from personal experience. Armstrong compares the multi-generation business with the family farm.

'You're stuck on it,' he observes. 'You all have to work there and wait until Dad dies or something. You've got to work together. All the capital is there, and there's no income. So you're really stuck. But a lot of family shareholdings are like that.'

The tight structure means that everybody is locked into the business. On the one hand, there are intense conflicts between family members. On the other hand, the members present a united front to the world. Hence the torn narrative of Harold Jackson, as he opens up about the troubled relationships in his family and then reflexively closes down again.

At the same time, the tight structure is inherently unstable. Interviewees use the language of war to describe the deterioration of family relationships as conflicts become more intense. Harold Jackson says he has been 'battered with this family approach'. Liz Turner speaks of going into 'combat mode'. Another interviewee talks about the family's 'Desert Storm'. In some cases, the dynasty explodes in public view, with the furious intensity of pent-up rage; first in the courts and then in the media. There has been a steady stream of celebrated dynastic explosions. The most famous was the Fairfax family in the 1980s; the most recent the Moran family and the Belgiorno-Nettis family.

One interviewee whose family business blew apart — I will call him Alexander Waterman — describes the explosion as a great release. Waterman was not the person who lit the fuse, but if someone else had not lit it then, the explosion would have eventually happened anyway. 'There was no doubt in my mind. If it wasn't going to be me, it would be my children. There would be a parting of the ways.'

For his part, Waterman has no dynastic ambitions for his own children. 'I don't think there should be an obligation for them to come in here [into the business] after me, or do anything like that. They're individuals. They've got a life to lead.'

Some of the people I interview are trying to find new ways of ensuring the survival of the family business in the face of individuals' ambitions. Following the example of big family businesses in the United States, they are setting up new processes — family meetings, family retreats, family councils and family constitutions. Such processes make the business more transparent and accountable to its stakeholders. Family constitutions, for example, specify the conditions under which family members can join the business or sell their stake in it. The processes also make the business more democratic — less at the behest of the patriarch and more accountable to all stakeholders. Democracy and accountability promote trust. Family members have a system whereby they can ventilate their grievances and seek redress. Trust prolongs the life of the business and defuses dynastic explosions.

At the same time, some of the patriarchs I interview, such as Harold Jackson, can barely conceal their contempt for these newer family business processes. They did not achieve their wealth by means of formal rules and procedures. On the contrary, they were rule-breakers, driving roughshod over formal procedures. And they are reluctant to hand over authority to the next generation.

'The more the shareholders are told,' Jackson grumbles, 'the more dissatisfied they become.'

'These family meetings are a terrible waste of time,' another man complains. 'I go along with them but some family members just do not understand the business.'

Only a few of the people I meet have successfully introduced formal family business processes. Consider, for example, Bill McAdam (not his real name). McAdam recalls reaching a point at

> 'I MEAN, IF YOU TALK TO MY BROTHERS, THEY JUST THINK IT'S THAT MUCH NONSENSE. THEY DON'T EVEN WANT TO HEAR ABOUT IT!'

which he realised that if he didn't get good professional management assistance his business would struggle forever. He successfully recruited professional managers, who helped the business to 'forge ahead and be on the cutting edge'.

Then McAdam faced the problem of bringing his children into the business. 'I knew it wasn't going to work,' he explains, 'unless there was a very good understanding of the conditions in place. I knew if I brought my son in to displace a professional that we already had in the business, he would be resisted, absolutely.'

McAdam introduced family meetings at which the family stakeholders discussed the issue of children joining the business. 'The major part of the interest in those discussions has been how you bring the next generation into the existing business without upsetting the existing staff. How do you bring in a member to take somebody else's slot? Do you just wait until a slot opens up, or would you displace somebody when it is convenient for the family? What does that do to staff morale?'

These meetings resulted in a family constitution, which included the conditions under which children could join the business. For example, they could not join it automatically. They had to work outside the family business for at least four years. 'They have to present their performance appraisals,' McAdam says, 'from whatever business they have been working in. They'll get evaluated!'

McAdam's children eventually did join the business and he is happy with the way it has worked out. The current plan, he explains, is to give his children exposure to all areas of the business. That way they will eventually be the automatic choice for the top job, 'because they'll have such a breadth of knowledge of the business over and above the other staff members'.

McAdam is passionate about keeping the business in the family. He has gone to a lot of trouble to bring his children into it, and his eyes mist over as he describes their decision to come on board. Even so, he is doubtful that the family business will survive for another generation. The 'next generation of cousins' will have to find ways of working together. They will 'marry lawyers or accountants or other professionals who will want to get out and take their share'. Divorces might create a further drain on the business. In other words, the personal ambitions and preferences of individual family members will militate against the evolution of a dynasty. Family business processes at least provide a vehicle for this to occur in a controlled way.

'The likelihood of family businesses surviving beyond a few generations in today's environment is highly unlikely,' McAdam reflects. 'I'm a realist: ours is not going to survive forever. The pressures will be such that — at some point of time — it will be pulled apart.'

Chapter Six

Inheritance

Secrets of the super rich

> 'MINE WILL GO ON FOREVER, AS FAR AS I'M CONCERNED. IT WILL BE ONE OF THOSE FORTUNES THAT WILL MULTIPLY INDEFINITELY!'

Bill Pease — the name is a pseudonym — was determined to improve on his parent's standard of living; they had only made a 'bare living'. Pease achieved his goal. He tells the story of how he passed from youthful entrepreneurial ventures, to his own businesses, and then to an array of investments. 'I'd always wanted to make money,' he says. 'I tried anything.'

Pease is disarmingly straightforward about the tension between making his fortune and taking care of his family. 'Well, you neglect your family life, that's for sure,' he says. 'I did. I've always been a worker. Work has always been my preference. But by having a successful business, I've been able to provide for my children and give them everything they've wanted. I look after them the best that I can. 'So I've neglected them, but I've provided for them for the rest of their lives. They can't have it both ways!'

Nowadays Pease describes himself as a one-man band. He runs a private investment empire with the support of professional managers. He invests heavily in property. 'It was something easy that didn't require a lot of work,' he explains. 'Nothing like collecting rent, I've always thought!' And he's proud of his empire and his fortune. 'I have a feeling of satisfaction in what I've done with my life. I feel that I've made a mark on the country, more so than lots of other people — although it has probably been more for myself.'

I ask Pease about the role of his children in the empire. This brings him around to his second story, the story of what will happen to his fortune after his death. He has thought a lot about this issue and is proud of what he has worked out. I think this may be why he has agreed to the interview.

'Well,' he says, 'I've been working on my estate planning for, I suppose, ten or fifteen years. That's the course I've taken.' He comments on what he believes is the normal course of events following the death of someone who has made a lot of money in their time. 'From what I can see, the sons and daughters come in, and they start to get upset and they can't run the bloody business. But mine will go on forever, as far as I'm concerned. It will be one of those fortunes that will multiply indefinitely!'

Pease explains why he started his estate planning. He says he couldn't see anyone in the family who was capable of filling his shoes. 'My children have never shown any inclination. They've never been sufficiently motivated or capable of input. Except for my daughter, who has spent time in the office, but now has two young children and is busy raising a family.'

Pease reflects for a moment. 'I've got too much wealth! If I said to any of my children, "Here's $10 million", I think they wouldn't know what to do with it. They wouldn't be capable of controlling it. And when they've got hundreds of millions of dollars, it's a bigger problem still.'

Besides doubting his children's ability to manage the fortune, Pease distrusted those who might marry his children — and in due course their children. 'My daughter is married to an outsider, for instance,' he says, 'and I look after her. He hangs on there, of course — he lives with her. She gets everything she wants. But he can't afford to keep her the way she lives, which is only natural, I suppose.'

It's revealing that Pease describes his son-in-law as an 'outsider'. He is determined that the son-in-law will not be able to get his hands on the fortune. 'I don't want to restrict [my daughter's] way of life,' he says. 'But if they divorce, well, she virtually hasn't got anything. She doesn't have assets or anything. She just gets an income from what I give her.

'So I think, if she gets a divorce, well, she'd split up what she's got, which is a few hundred thousand dollars — and that's it, as I see it. That's what I'm led to believe.'

Pease has created a structure whereby the business — following his death — will be managed by an outside board of directors with one family representative. Pease's children will not be able to come in and manage the business. Nor will they be able to sell it. The fortune will be locked away. The board will distribute entitlements to Pease's children and his lineal descendants, and also to charities.

'The straight-out lineal descendants receive an entitlement for whatever they want, while they're living,' he explains. 'But their spouses don't,' he adds. 'They don't get anything.'

I wonder about the long-term effects of this type of succession planning. Bill Pease's descendants will always have a guaranteed flow of easy money. How will this affect their lives? I ask Pease whether he is worried about this issue.

'Oh, I think that it's going to ruin them all,' he says ironically, 'but still . . .'

He laughs and so do I. There are worse ways to be ruined.

'It's something they can live with,' he resumes. 'I suppose there'll be one or two along the way who'll do well. Some won't.'

Pease has thought about how to deal with the ones who do not do so well. There is an inside board of family directors to monitor how family members spend the money. 'If you've got someone who's a no-hoper, well, he won't get anything. They'll restrict what he gets.'

I ask Pease whether he knows anybody else with a similar succession plan. He doesn't — but he does have a model in mind. 'I just think that it's something like the Rockefeller Foundation and these types of things. They're big families and they've managed to keep going, without any particular Rockefeller running the show. I think this will go on in the same way.'

It's not just the family that will keep going across the generations, it's also the fortune. 'I think we've got the perfect system,' Pease tentatively suggests, 'but I don't know.'

Deborah Bryant (an assumed name) inherited her wealth. Most of the people I've interviewed are self-made and I'm keen to interview Bryant because I want to extend my horizons, to find out something about the experience of inherited wealth.

'I CALL IT MY SECRET LIFE.'

For her part, Bryant is very cautious about being interviewed. 'This money has brought so much pain to my family,' she says on the telephone.

Bryant hates being on the Rich Lists. She tells me that the family wealth was never 'public knowledge' in earlier times. It was not even common knowledge in the family.

'We never really knew when we were young. It wasn't really talked about — I think my parents were in denial about it. They didn't really want to know about it and didn't want us to feel different.

'But there was always a sense of: There's some money there somewhere!'

Bryant has rebelled against her inheritance and her class. As a teenager she went to all the right parties and met all the right people. She reels off the household names of tycoons, politicians and celebrities. 'I just felt so uncomfortable,' she says. 'It was just not my scene at all — to be among people who were obviously quite relishing the fact that they would be the future movers and shakers in Macquarie Street and on the Stock Exchange, and wherever they wanted to go, really. There was such a sense of ease — that doors would be opened everywhere. I felt the injustice of it quite keenly.'

Bryant describes the world of exclusive private schools, yacht clubs and parties. She always felt very uncomfortable among the plummy English accents, and the intangible social barriers keeping out the common types. 'It felt unreal. You know, during my twenties there were times when I was thinking, I'm mad! How am I going to end up, because I am going to become incredibly wealthy! How is that going to work out in my life, because I don't want that wealth! I don't want that to be in the way of my relating to people.'

Inherited wealth, she adds, causes all manner of problems for families and individuals. She talks about the idle rich — the people who haven't worked at making it, but have it. 'It might seem like an enviable position, but I think it's very difficult for your self-esteem. This life is very much oriented around people gaining status through what they do.' Moreover: 'Having lots of money gives you lots of choices, which is a great thing, but having lots of choices can be absolutely paralysing. There are so many choices that it can just overwhelm you.'

When Bryant turned 21, she started receiving dividends from the family estate. The dividends were money for nothing. They were not welcome. 'They came each year, these dividends. I was hugely against them, because I felt that capital gain was totally fucked. From the word go, I started giving the money away. I was vehement about it. Absolutely defiant about it!'

Bryant has been giving money away ever since. As she tries to explain what is involved in giving money away, she stumbles over words and metaphors, occasionally becoming tongue-tied. It's 'a really bizarre situation'. It can be 'a full-time job', scouting out projects and organisations that will use the money effectively. It can be a 'trap', because in trying to escape the effects of an inheritance you spend all of your time thinking about it. 'It's a bit like a secret life, really.' Later she repeats herself: 'I call it my secret life.'

The phrase — 'my secret life' — catches my ear. I ask Bryant why it has to be that way.

'I wish I didn't have to be secretive about it,' she replies. 'I wish I didn't have to *not* tell people about it, because it is actually quite a big bit of my life and it takes up a lot of my head space. I've discovered, through experience really, that it does affect how people view me and get to know me.

'It's the last taboo. I mean, money is just the last taboo. It's something that most people are trying to get more of in their lives these days. Most people are working really hard to make big bucks — and I've got a whole heap of them.'

People behave differently towards Bryant once they know of her wealth. She compartmentalises her life to protect herself, yet she is on the horns of a dilemma. She rebelled against her inheritance because she didn't want money to get in the way of her relationships. She wanted authentic relationships, but as soon as she's open about her inheritance, people are unable to see past her money. She tells close friends about her secret life, but finds it takes a long time to do so and requires deep trust. Even then, it puts strain on the relationship. 'We try to be as honest with each other as we can and most people say, "Yeah, I'm really jealous. I'm working really hard. If I had money like that, I would buy a house. I would buy myself the drum kit that I've always wanted."

'People want money, and I've got a whole lot of it. I think that inequality is difficult in a relationship — any kind of relationship. Class is a difficult thing. Class is a difficult thing.'

It is much easier for Bryant to form relationships where inequality is not an issue. Yet this pathway takes her back to where she began — with people from privileged backgrounds. Bryant has found a 'community' of other women who also have big fortunes and a social conscience. She was 'totally and utterly relieved' when she did so, not least because she could talk about what was on her mind without being guarded. 'People get together,' she explains, 'and talk about the projects they're doing and what they're giving money to. You know, it's quite a support group.'

Bryant's siblings do not confront these dilemmas. They have, she says, 'big houses, big holiday houses, and they have very different lives from me'. Their children attend Cranbrook and Shore. 'They are actually upper class now, they all mix in totally upper-class circles. They mix with other people of similar income. No, not similar *income*; they mix with other people who have *inherited* money. That's who they mix with.

'So that's all very comfortable, because they're all in the same boat and they can afford to do the same things.'

Bryant is not so comfortable, because she keeps jumping boats. Eventually she plans to do so for good and give away all of her inherited fortune. Then she will no longer require a secret life. Yet she worries that her children will one day make comparisons with their wealthy cousins. '"How come my cousins are getting to fly to Hawaii for their holidays? Why can't I do that?" That's going to be difficult.'

She also worries about her own welfare. 'I'm anxious about it already. I really don't want to regret it. I don't want to be in dire straits — giving all this money to all these things. Like, you'd kick yourself, wouldn't you! You'd certainly lose a bit of sleep!'

Bill Pease states that nobody really wants to be on the Rich Lists. Certainly most of the people I interview object to them. There are two main objections.

First, the lists, in Deborah Bryant's words, 'make you a target'. Rich people are powerful but they are also vulnerable. The lists provide a short cut for individuals and organisations — from charities to criminals to taxation officials — who want to identify and locate rich people for one reason or another. Overwhelmingly they want to tap some of the wealth.

'WHAT DID YOU DO TO GET THAT MONEY? NOTHING!'

'If you're rich,' says one man, 'nearly everybody is chasing you for a dollar!'

There are good reasons for keeping a 'secret life'.

Second, getting listed transforms the public identity of interviewees — and their families. When Valerie Wilson conducted focus groups on the subject of personal money for her book *The Secret Life of Money*, she found that she had to run groups whose individual members earned approximately the same income. Otherwise people wouldn't talk, feeling uncomfortable about being too rich or uncomfortable about being too poor.

In everyday life, people handle economic differences through secrecy and discretion. They do so because — among other reasons — economic differences are imbued with moral meanings. Some cultural traditions, such as the Protestant work ethic, Social Darwinism and the American-style entrepreneurial ethos, present wealth as a measure of personal worth as rewarded by the markets. Wealth is the product of hard work and thrift, or initiative and imagination, or risk and daring, or whatever. Other traditions, such as Christian asceticism, socialism and Australian egalitarianism, regard wealth as the outcome of greed, exploitation and bastardry.

Often the people I interview contrast the moral meanings attached to wealth in the United States with those in Australia. In the United States, says one man, 'you're respected for the amount of money you have'. There is a 'philosophy of rags to riches'. In Australia the philosophy is the opposite. 'People won't respect you because you've got money. In fact, they actually look down on you. You're a tall poppy. They want to shoot you.'

'There is a general feeling in Australia,' says another man, 'that if you are rich you're a ruthless lying bastard — the so-called tall poppy syndrome.'

The Rich Lists are not discreet. They blast secrecy and discretion out of the water. They blast through the taboos around personal wealth. The lists label individuals and families as 'super rich' whether they like it or not. They define people in terms of their wealth alone — as 'someone who has a huge fortune'. In the process they transform the most routine aspects of everyday life. One man describes how the Rich Lists spoiled his going for a swim at the local beach. 'Until eighteen months ago, I could go quietly about my life. No one knew what I did or what I was worth. And what changed? All that changed was that something was written in a magazine.

'To people, you're money! You're not who you were yesterday. Somehow, you're someone different.'

At the same time, self-made men and women are often ambivalent about the Rich Lists. They are proud of their achievements for which the lists provide some social recognition. One man describes a secretive pleasure in being on the lists. Most people, he says, claim that they do not want to be listed.

'But quietly they'll sit on the toilet, and read the thing, and say, "Oh, I'm higher than him this year!"'

The same man goes on to admit that he is quite proud to be on the list, having come to Australia with nothing. He believes that there has been a sea change in Australian attitudes to wealth, which makes the recognition of the Rich Lists more comfortable than it used to be. More people own shares; more people admire wealth.

'Here I am,' he reflects, 'sitting on a pile of assets — which is beyond belief to me — and so, in an odd way, I'm quite happy to be known as well off.'

In contrast, people who have inherited their wealth express no pleasure in the Rich Lists. Deborah Bryant, for example, takes no pride in her listing.

'I think that, in our culture, there's definitely this sense that you should make your own money. You're allowed to be rich if you've made your own money, and that's what everybody aspires to do.

'But if you've somehow got it because someone else made it for you, then that's not quite kosher. What did you do to get that money? Nothing! So somehow it's not seen as right, and I can understand that.'

An interviewee with inherited wealth — I will call him Graeme Anderson — bristles when I ask him about his 'establishment' background. These days, Anderson says, 'coming from an establishment background is used as a negative: "He's from an establishment family, therefore ..."' His voice trails off in frustration.

'Does it irritate you?' I ask.

'Completely,' he replies emphatically. 'I mean, I regard myself as much a self-made person as any other. There are a lot of people from my background who've completely disappeared. As you said earlier, it's often harder to build a business if you have a well-off background than if you haven't.'

Secrets of the super rich

It was once a source of social honour to come from an old family. The new rich in the late nineteenth and early twentieth centuries clambered to attain the social status and the lifestyle of old families. I am struck by the fact that Anderson distances himself from his 'well-off background', prefering to describe himself as 'self-made'. Self-made wealth is more prestigious than an inherited fortune. People with inherited wealth live in the shadow of their fortune: the shadow covers them with a sense of shame.

> 'NEARLY ALL THE WEALTH WAS IN THE BUSINESS. YOU COULDN'T RISK IT FOREVER.'

Among self-made entrepreneurs, the desire for a dynasty is often powerful, yet they are frequently reluctant to pursue that aspiration at any cost. There are four reasons. First, entrepreneurs worry that business dynasties are bad for children. Harold Clough, for example, tells me that he was put off by the fact that he still remembered how his father and he had fought. 'But also,' he says, if your kids come into your business, they're always treated differently.

'Half the staff will treat them extra nicely, because they're the boss's son or daughter, and half the staff will treat them extra tough, because they're the boss's son or daughter. But no one treats them normally.'

More generally, interviewees emphasise the principles of individual choice and personal fulfilment, over and above the principle of dynastic succession.

'As far as my views on dynasties go,' Gerry Harvey says, 'I think that everyone's an individual, and they should do whatever they want to do.'

'My ambitions,' one matriarch says of her children, 'are for them to achieve their optimum potential in whatever area they choose.'

'I think that we're individuals,' another interviewee comments, 'and we all have different goals, aspirations and preferences.

'This business of trying to harness them, or putting them in some shape or form, isn't realistic. I mean, we're moving into a very individualistic age, I think.'

A second reason for the reluctance of family heads to pursue a dynasty at any cost is the principle of equal inheritance among children, including daughters. Some patriarchs still adopt the dynastic strategy of earlier times. Liz Turner's father is leaving his business to his boy. At one time, daughters accepted this situation — it was the way things were. But no longer. The earlier strategy now involves big risks — disaffected daughters, legal disputes, family breakdown and public humiliation.

The people I interview overwhelmingly accept the principle of equal inheritance. They justify it on the grounds of fairness and family cohesion. 'In my will,' says one man carefully, 'my total assets are left to my wife. Apart from three or four personal bequests, she controls the whole lot of it. Then, when she dies, it goes equally to the two children. I don't know of any better way.'

'If you give it on the basis of anything other than equal,' says another man, 'I think you will create the breakdown of the family of the next generation.'

Third, entrepreneurs are reluctant to pursue a dynasty at any cost because they fear that it is bad for the business. They worry that bringing their children into the business might put it — and the fortune — at risk. 'My children have never shown any inclination,' Bill Pease says. 'They've never been sufficiently motivated or capable of input.'

Apart from anything else, the scale of the business makes it increasingly difficult to bring children into management. For example, John Wilcox (a pseudonym) recalls joining his father's business. 'I worked closely with my father,' he explains. 'The company, at the time

I got involved, was fairly small. We probably had a staff of only about twenty people or something of that nature. There was no management structure as such. He was the boss; everyone else was the worker. You know, the opportunity to work at his right hand was there.'

This is no longer the case. Wilcox says he now has a fairly large organisation with an excellent management team. He adds, 'It is very difficult to bring a son or daughter into a senior management position, where they would become the heir apparent and be able to continue the dynasty, as it were.'

Finally, entrepreneurs are tempted to sell off the business in any case, in order to protect — or as one man puts it, to 'stabilise' — the fortune. 'When you're 25,' he says, 'you don't have much to lose. When you're 30, you have a bit more, and so it goes. When you get to my age, and if you make a mistake, you have a fair bit to lose.'

'You don't want to go broke at any stage of your life,' says another man. 'But if you go broke at 35 you think, I've got all those years ahead of me: I can be back on top again and going.

'If you go broke at 65 you think, Well, that's it. I've got no chance of recovery. So you tend, I think, to lose some of that entrepreneurial spirit.'

Entrepreneurs fear the instability of markets. The winner-take-all economy means that fortunes can be won and lost very quickly. Bob Clifford's changing fortunes in the shipbuilding industry are a case in point. Entrepreneurs such as Clifford mostly make their money in one business, in the one line of industry. As the business grows, all of their wealth is concentrated in the one business. All of their eggs are in the one basket: entrepreneurs protect their fortunes by spreading their exposure to risk. They spread the eggs over many different baskets.

For example, Paul O'Brien (an assumed name) describes how he was in a 'high-risk business and a highly capital-intensive industry'. The business was growing fast.

Inheritance

'When you're a smaller size,' O'Brien reflects, 'you work like hell to try to build up and you have all your money in one asset or one business. When you get over a certain size, then you've got to stand back and say, "Does that still make sense?"' O'Brien's business had reached the point where it required a massive capital injection — hundreds of millions of dollars. 'Even if we could have raised that amount of money, it would've been crazy for us to do so — the risks become too high.'

Similarly, Nick Balagiannis, who made his money manufacturing poker machines, says that selling the business was a very hard decision. 'Coming from a very poor family, we didn't have any other wealth. Nearly all the wealth was in the business. You couldn't risk it forever. It was time to take some money out — you know, playing it safe. In that manner, we thought that we could live very comfortably. My partner was also getting a little bit tired. We thought, Let it go!'

Balagiannis cashed up on his business, but says he is now working harder than ever. He reflects that if he put the money in the bank then he would have plenty of time for leisure. But if he did this he would eventually go broke, 'because the money would vanish in the bank'. Better to invest in different types of solid properties and businesses, he reflects. Balagiannis is building his investment portfolio, which takes time. 'It takes a lot of time to put it together and manage it. Until you find the right people to manage it for you, it's not an easy task. It's starting from scratch again!'

Other interviewees have their investment companies in place. One man, for example, comments that he runs his private investment company like a public company. He has wide-ranging investments in office buildings, shopping centres, cattle stations, public companies, and venture capital projects. 'We're not lenders in the normal sense,' he explains, 'because we're not lending money at the relatively low rate that the banks get for it. But we will lend high-cost money and take a piece of the action, if we like the deal.'

Similarly, Bill Pease describes his preference for property. 'Nothing like collecting rent, I've always thought!' he says.

> 'THEY'RE ALL GOOD, HARD-WORKING PEOPLE, BUT THEY JUST DON'T THINK TWICE ABOUT HAVING FUN.'

James Armstrong — as I have called him — observes that wealthy families, when they're setting up in a generational sense, move away from the original business towards investment companies with very loose structures. 'They move to structures which are much broader investment companies. You've seen the Lowys do it. The Myers have done it. They've built investment companies outside their core business, and that's for flexibility.

'At the end of the day, you can foresee that in a generation's time the original business is almost irrelevant.'

In other words, diversification not only stabilises the fortune, it also paves the way for leaving the *money* to the children, rather than leaving them the *business*. Family members will not be stuck in a family company — or in a 'tight structure', as Armstrong puts it. The family wealth will be fluid and flexible: easy to divide into equal portions for the next generation — sons *and* daughters — and easy for individual family members to take their money and make their own way in the world.

Take for example Harold Clough, who inherited a small building business from his father and built an international civil engineering and construction company. Clough first thought about floating the business in the 1970s and over the next 25 years revisited the idea about a dozen times, but each time decided they were better off remaining private than they were going public. In the mid-1990s he finally did float the business, mainly for reasons of succession. It meant that his children would eventually be able to realise their personal shareholdings 'easily and reasonably and fairly'.

A family company now holds the family stake in the public company. The board of directors for the family company includes all of Clough's children — sons and daughters. One of the issues under consideration is how much of the family's assets should be tied up in one entity.

'If you go to any financial advisor,' Clough says, 'he'll tell you, "Don't have all your eggs in one basket". If we followed that advice, we'd sell out most of our shares in the company. But emotionally, a number of the family members don't want us to do that. The staff don't want us to do that. I don't particularly want us to do that. So while I'm the head of the family that won't happen. But when I die...' He looks away, then revises his estimate. 'I'd be surprised if, within another decade or even less, they didn't sell down the shares in the company quite substantially.'

Paul O'Brien, another second-generation entrepeneur, sold the family business lock, stock and barrel. He had to consider not only his sons and daughters but also his nephews and nieces. 'They're all going to want to do their own thing,' he reflects. 'Some will want to go into the business; some will want to go and do other things.

'We believed that, in the longer term, it wasn't fair to have them all dependent on one family business and have some working in it and some not in it. The potential problems of that! We didn't know what they'd be, but we saw that there would be potential problems in the future.'

Andrew Kellahear (not his real name) has also sold the family business. He explains that the family wealth is now held in family trusts. He still singlemindedly pursues business opportunities. 'I've got more things going on than I've ever had in my life,' he says. 'It keeps me going. So I suppose that's my life.

'To go on and have nothing on my plate would drive me mad. I thought about five or six years ago that I was going to slow down, but I've *increased*.'

Kellahear still controls the family trusts, redirecting the money into new ventures as he sees fit. 'But on my death it changes,' he says. 'I'm only worried about it while I'm here.'

The fortune will be divided among his sons and daughters. 'I wouldn't dream of treating them differently,' he remarks.

And he is philosophical about the future of the fortune. There will *not* be a dynasty.

'They'll lose it pretty quickly, I'm perfectly sure!' he says. 'They'll get $30 million each, say. It'll be interesting to see what happens. They won't regard it as I do, that's for sure!'

Kellahear suddenly becomes aware of his words. He interrupts himself. 'But they're all good people!' he emphasises. 'No one is on drugs or anything. They're all good, hard-working people, but they just don't think twice about having fun. It's a fun life!'

> 'IT IS A BLOODY BIG WORRY! IT IS A BLOODY BIG WORRY, YEAH. IT'S A VERY BIG WORRY.'

Telling me about his upbringing, the son of a Holocaust survivor describes being imbued with a very strong work ethic. 'Never rest on your laurels,' he adds. 'Always think that someone is going to come and take from you what you've got.'

When I ask him about his own children, he quotes his father, who told him once that 'the rich were the first to die in the war'. He ponders that, then says, 'Wealth is a fleeting thing. You'll find that the people who no longer have it thought they were going to have it forever.

'I want to make sure that the kids have a work ethic, know the value of money, understand that you don't get it without working for it, that you can work for it and still not have it, and that you've got to have self-sufficiency from within to survive in this world.'

This is a common refrain. The super rich are routinely concerned about the motivation of their children and their ability to hold on to the fortune. The issue crops up again and again in the course of interviews.

'I think I have one advantage over my children,' says one man. 'I know about economic deprivation.'

'You see, if you're brought up with money,' says another man, 'you don't know what it's like with no money.'

'It's a battle between giving them a high-quality experience and taking away their motivation,' says another.

The super rich attach conditions to their estate in line with the extent to which they want to protect their fortune against their children. The bottom line is that the children have never done the 'hard yards'. The super rich often fear that their children will squander the fortune; alternatively, they fear that avaricious spouses or 'outsiders' will ravage it.

Interviewees are sometimes coy about the conditions attached to their estate. Moreover, my middle-class upbringing fails to alert me properly to this useful line of inquiry: my questions are not penetrating. Even so, at least three interviewees tell me how they have devised legal structures so that their children will *never* get the money. They are especially concerned about the future of their fortune.

For example, Bill Pease has protected his fortune, for now and forever. Similarly, another man worries about the possibility of divorce among his children and later descendants. 'It's a bloody big worry, a very big worry,' he says. 'Even in my will, I don't leave money to my children. I leave it in the trust. They don't get it straight.'

'How long before they do get it?' I ask uncertainly.

'They never get it,' he replies. He explains how the trust makes it more difficult for spouses to 'attack' the fortune. Then he repeats himself. 'It is a bloody big worry! It is a bloody big worry, yeah. It's a very big worry.'

There is another point. By implication, a protective trust guarantees that the family will keep going. The founder of the fortune will loom over future generations, shaping the contours of their lives. Future generations will be obliged to maintain contact with each other, managing the dispersal of funds. It will be a dynasty of sorts.

> 'IF YOU GIVE THEM $20 MILLION OR $200 MILLION, I THINK IT'S A CURSE POTENTIALLY.'

On the one hand, interviewees fear that their children will lose the fortune. On the other, they also fear that the fortune will spoil their children.

'I just hope it doesn't bugger up their lives,' says one man ruefully, 'because I'd hate it. That would be the worst legacy that you could ever leave your kids!'

Interviewees worry that their children will lack initiative because they have not had to struggle and make their own way in the world. They worry that their children will not value themselves, knowing that they live off the wealth of their parents. And they worry that their children will not lead 'normal' lives — that they'll be cut off from everyday social relationships by their wealth.

For example, Gerald Singer — an assumed name — warns that children need to have their own skills and their own sense of values. He talks about how rich families in the United States 'went totally discombobulated' — with disasters for the individuals. 'I think, in a nutshell, if you give your children $2 million or something, it's a boon. They can buy a house, or they can put it away and have an investment or so on. But if you give them $20 million or $200 million, I think it's a curse potentially, because it is so out of whack — out of all proportion — to anything that normal people come across.

'So it's a dilemma!'

Deborah Bryant, who inherited her fortune, feels much the same. She says, 'Having lots of choices can be absolutely paralysing.' Inherited wealth might seem enviable, but 'it's very difficult for your self-esteem'. She struggles to establish authentic relationships beyond a circle of other people with inherited fortunes. Then she feels bad about feeling bad. 'It's something that you don't feel you can talk to many people about. What right have I to go, "Oh God, life is so hard with all this money"?'

There is a simple solution to these dilemmas. Give the money away! Gerald Singer and Deborah Bryant are both adopting this solution. And another four interviewees insist that they will eventually leave their fortune to worthy causes rather than to their children.

'The money — like, you can't spend that much money,' says one of the younger entrepreneurs. 'Actually it's dangerous, and people who haven't earned it . . .' He pauses, then tells me it would be a sad thing to give it all to his children, adding that he plans to give it back to the community somehow. 'That will be in the second half of my life, hopefully,' he remarks.

Giving the money away is a brave solution, but it is also nerve-racking. While inherited wealth might have its problems, it sure beats poverty! Giving the money away might seem like a good idea now, but what will it seem like further down the track? And what will the next generation think about it?

'I'm anxious about it already,' Bryant says. 'I'm anxious about it and I really don't want to regret it.'

Similarly, Singer emphasises the difficulty of the decision. 'Let me tell you,' he says, 'that it is the hardest thing — one of the hardest things — that I've ever done, because when you give it you're actually giving it — it's gone.' He returns to the difficulty of the decision throughout the interview. It has been 'a hell of a job psychologically', given the financial hardship of his parents and grandparents. It is 'scary'. He has worked hard for his fortune. It is his security. 'If you fall on hard times, nobody is going to give it back to you.' He feels 'quite insecure, crazy as it might sound'. The difficulty of the decision is a measure of how much Singer is swimming against the tide.

He describes an internal dialogue whereby he confronts his fears. 'So what it has done,' he says, 'is that it has made me actually say to myself, "Now, I've got to be more gutsy in myself and my own ability — not to just keep what I've got or to make it bigger, but if something bad happens, to fix it."'

A moment later he quotes another internal dialogue. 'I say to myself, "The more that I give, the happier I feel about myself and the more I can look at myself in the mirror and say, you're okay."'

A month or so after the interview I send Singer a transcript. The words of his reply are playful, belying the seriousness of his concerns. 'I am delighted with the content (naturally!),' he writes, 'and found little fault with the quality of the interviewee's philosophy!' He has taken more than usual care in editing the transcript, although he has not changed the meaning of what he said. He asks for a copy of the final transcript, which he says he will keep for the future generations of his family. My guess is that he wants them to understand *why* he did what he did with the money. He wants them to know that he was okay.

Chapter Seven

Old families

Secrets of the super rich

> 'WE GOT THROUGH A GREAT DEAL OF LIQUOR AND MONEY, AND DAD SAID THE MONEY DIDN'T MATTER, I COULD SPEND WHAT I LIKED, AND I CERTAINLY DID.'

William ('Big') Clarke was the Kerry Packer of nineteenth century Australia. He was the richest man in the land, and the only Australian with a 'world-class fortune' comparable to the great fortunes being assembled in the United States.

Clarke arrived in Australia from the English county of Somerset in 1829. His father, a yeoman farmer, had died when Clarke was still a teenager and a few years later the young man had decided to emigrate, encouraged by the belief that the Australian climate would be good for his weak chest. He made his way to Hobart and set up as a butcher. He was a big man with a long, pockmarked face, a limp arising from a congenitally deformed hip, and rough manners. Above all, he was an accumulator, relentlessly acquiring land, sheep and cattle — first in Van Diemen's Land and then in Victoria, South Australia and New Zealand. His reputation for accumulation was matched only by his reputation for meanness. He gave nothing away.

In the 1850s Clarke followed his principal investments, moving from Hobart to Melbourne. He also diversified his portfolio, becoming a big shareholder and a director of the Colonial Bank. In his later years 'Big' Clarke became so big that his deformed hip could no longer bear his weight. It took four men to carry him to and from his carriage for meetings at the bank.

Clarke died in 1874, leaving £2.5 million. Even then the Melbourne press felt no reason to show respect. One newspaper observed: 'His widespread reputation ... was not the result of a public career of usefulness, but was consequent on his wealth ... His one object in life was to make money.' Another obituary commented on his parsimonious habits. A third poked fun at the provision for illegitimate children in his will.

'Big' Clarke left the best part of his fortune — about £1.5 million — to his eldest son William and a substantial share to his third son Joseph, both of whom were active in the business. The second son, Thomas, was excluded from the business affairs of the estate, as were Clarke's estranged wife and his illegitimate children.

'Thomas wasn't trusted by 'Big' Clarke,' a descendant observed, 'because he kept hounds and a park full of deer — he lived the life of a country squire.'

Whereas 'Big' Clarke was an accumulator, the younger William was a spender. The American writer Thorstein Veblen coined the term 'conspicuous consumption' to describe the ostentatious spending habits of the new American rich in the late nineteenth century. He could easily have been writing about the younger William Clarke.

First, William gave credit where credit was due. He built a grand vault for his father, with a 38-foot (11.4-metre) Gothic spire. Then, with the encouragement of his second wife Janet, he built a huge mansion at Sunbury, named 'Rupertswood' after his first-born son. The Clarkes entertained in lavish style there, with guests arriving in their hundreds at a private railway station. They often entertained the guests with martial displays by their private artillery. The couple were also great benefactors and philanthropists. In 1882 William Clarke was rewarded with a baronetcy from Queen Victoria.

Sir William and his wife were undisputed leaders of colonial society. They were rich, powerful and respectable. Sir William was first President of the Melbourne Football Association, President of the Melbourne Cricket Club, Commodore of the Royal Victorian Yacht Squadron, and first Grand Master of the United Grand Lodge of Victoria. He also followed his father as a representative in the Victorian Legislative Council and on the board of the Colonial Bank. In 1888, at the peak of an economic boom, the family moved to Cliveden, a grand mansion in East Melbourne with 28 bedrooms; there were 17 rooms for indoor servants. The mansion became the focal point for high society in the colony.

The Clarke fortune prospered in the 1880s boom but suffered heavily in the 1893 bank crash. The strain contributed to Sir William's sudden death from a heart attack in 1897. He left an estate valued at £1 million, distributed among his widow and ten surviving children. The fortune was still a great one, but it was less than half of what it had been.

The oldest son Rupert — educated at Oxford — became the second baronet, and inherited the largest share of his father's estate. Whereas Sir William had been a pillar of colonial society, Sir Rupert was a loose cannon. He took his father's place as Governor of the Colonial Bank and a Legislative Councillor — but only for a while. He drifted from one business venture to another. In 1909 his wife divorced him for adultery with the daughter of a butcher. On the outbreak of World War I, Sir Rupert, now in his late forties, joined up as a lieutenant in the British Army. He was discharged in 1917, after catching malaria in Greece.

Sir Rupert had two daughters by his first marriage. Phyllis, the eldest, told in her memoirs, *From These Descended*, how her father set her husband Reg up as a gentleman farmer, but the couple were unable to live within their means. Reg played polo with the Government House team, and Phyllis hosted a busy social life. 'We got through a great deal of liquor and money,' Phyllis wrote, 'and Dad said the money didn't matter, I could spend what I liked, and I certainly did.'

Then in 1918 Phyllis received the shocking news by telegram that her 51-year-old father was marrying one Elsie Tucker. She later recalled her reaction. 'Who was Elsie Tucker?' she wrote. 'I'd never heard of her, and it was several weeks before I heard she was a Sydney girl of twenty, who had been acting as my father's secretary. I wired the news to Poss [her sister], and her answer was typical of her: "Isn't Dad tiresome?"'

In 1919 Elsie — who later changed her name to Elise — gave birth to a male heir, named Rupert. The event was a turning point in Phyllis's own story. Sir Rupert warned Phyllis and Reg that they must live within their income, including Phyllis's allowance of £1500 per year. In 1926 Sir Rupert died suddenly and her allowance dried up altogether. 'To say that I was stunned,' Phyllis recalled, 'was an understatement. What was I to do? I had several thousand pounds worth of bills. How was I to meet them, and how were we to live?'

Phyllis dismissed the servants, sold the car and tried to sell her jewellery. The couple left their home and moved into 'rooms' with their former cook, who had bought a small weatherboard house in the 'working-class quarter' of Malvern, a Melbourne suburb. They occupied the three front rooms of the house. Phyllis and her daughter shared one bedroom; Reg occupied the other. 'We paid five pounds a week for all of us,' Phyllis wrote, 'and really were well fed.' Eventually the trustees of Sir Rupert's estate came good with £30 per month, whereupon Phyllis and Reg reclaimed precarious gentility in the elite suburb of Toorak.

Whereas Phyllis moved in with her cook, her young half-brother Rupert moved into his birthright. At the tender age of six he became the third baronet, and in due course attended Eton and Oxford. In contrast to his father, he was respectable and discreet. He had a distinguished career as a company director. His directorships included the National Bank — formerly the Colonial Bank — where he took his uncle's seat on the board in 1955, serving as chairman of the board in the tumultuous 1980s.

The journalist Keith Dunstan described Sir Rupert as 'shy, even inhibited'. He was a man who did not talk to the press. In contrast, his wife Lady Kathleen 'talks in a loud voice and every thought that comes into her head, both discreet and indiscreet, she lets loose in a wonderful non-stop scream'. Lady Kathleen talked happily to the press — and the press regularly consulted her whenever it ran a story about old money. For example, in one interview with Kristin Williamson, she told how she had brought nannies out from England when her children were young. 'They came from Miss Lightbody's, the same place that supplies the Queen,' she recalled. 'They supplied all the top families.'

In another interview Lady Kathleen confided to Jane Cadzow that she sometimes feared that one of her children might choose the wrong marriage partner. 'I'm a great believer in falling in love,' she explained. 'We were just very fortunate that they fell in love with the right people.' For example, her first-born son Rupert — the future fourth baronet — married Susannah Law-Smith. Susannah's father was Sir Robert Law-Smith, a former director of the National Bank and BHP. Her mother was Joan Darling, whose father was on the boards of both companies a generation earlier.

Yet the most consistent theme in Lady Kathleen's interviews was a sense of loss. There was 'no such thing as society any more'. In business there were 'very few people you can say are true blue'. She nostalgically recalled the days when Toorak was a cosy community of interconnected families, most of whom had large country properties as well. 'Everyone had big, big houses and big, big gardens and you *knew* everybody. Now everybody wants to live in Toorak — everybody who wants to think they're anybody. I mean, it's all changed. In those days it was terribly selective.'

The Clarke family featured in the *BRW* Rich Lists from 1987 to 1992, before its estimated fortune fell below the then qualification level of $40 million. The family was still rich, but it was no longer in the same league as the new fortunes. The family's fortune had run into the sand — ravaged early on by conspicuous consumption, and increasingly dispersed across the many children of successive generations.

Most nineteenth century fortunes ran into the sand. A few prospered. None of them prospered as much as the Fairfax family fortune. In the twenty-first century the Fairfaxes are still among the ranks of the super rich in Australia.

John Fairfax first assembled the fortune. In the mid-1830s he was the co-proprietor of the *Leamington Chronicle*, a weekly four-page broadsheet in the English spa town of Leamington. He was also a devout Dissenter — serious, independent and abstemious. One of his contemporaries later described him as 'pre-eminently the accomplished man of business and the faithful servant of Christ'. Fairfax believed — in accordance with Weber's Protestant work ethic

> 'FOR THE FIRST TIME IN MY LIFE, I'M ON MY OWN. I'M A PERSON IN MY OWN RIGHT RATHER THAN THE HEIR TO A DYNASTY.'

Secrets of the super rich

— that success in business followed devotion to the Lord. He often quoted the words, 'It is well, Sir, to be busy in both worlds.'

Fairfax's confidence in the Lord was severely tested by an expensive and protracted libel action. The action was unsuccessful, but the court costs bankrupted him. Fairfax decided to emigrate and arrived in Sydney in 1838, whereupon he joined the Congregational Church and found employment as a printer. Three years later he bought a half share in Sydney's only daily newspaper, the *Sydney Herald* — later the *Sydney Morning Herald*. The business prospered: Fairfax's confidence in the Lord was well rewarded.

When John Fairfax died in 1875, the Congregational minister who conducted the funeral service paid tribute above all to his industry. Fairfax, he observed, believed that the hours of the day were too precious to be wasted.

> 'Do all you can while you can' was one of the very last sentences that he put down upon paper, and it was an aphorism illustrated by the whole of his career. His industry was not fitful and intermittent, like the streams in Australia, that are dry in drought and in summer. It was more like one of the English rivers, ever flowing.

Fairfax's two surviving children, James Reading and Edward, already owned half of the business between them. Now they inherited the other half. The brothers immediately brought in a general manager to manage the day-to-day business, while they retained ultimate authority.

James Reading Fairfax was at the helm of the business for almost 50 years. It became a platform for his wider leadership in commerce and civil society. He was a director of the Bank of New South Wales, the AMP Society and the shipping company Burns Philp. He was a

Old families

life member of the executive committee of the Congregational Union of New South Wales and President of the Young Men's Christian Association. He was President of the Royal Sydney Golf Club and Commodore of the Royal Sydney Yacht Squadron. And more besides. In 1898 he was knighted for his efforts.

James Reading's younger brother Edward was more retiring. Twelve years after his father's death he decided, at the relatively early age of 47, to free himself from the cares of office 'in order to obtain leisure which might be devoted to other pursuits'. He retired to England. James Reading bought out his brother's share — 'pruning the family tree', so to speak, with control of the business again in the hands of one branch of the family.

Sir James Reading Fairfax died in 1919. He had six children — five sons and a daughter. The eldest son Charles had, like his uncle, retired to England; he got nothing from the will. Two sons, Geoffrey and James, who were in the family firm, were left the larger part (about three-quarters) of the business. The remaining quarter was divided among the other three children.

Geoffrey and James, the third generation, were two peas from the same pod. They attended Sydney Grammar and Oxford together. They both left the nonconformist Congregational Church for the establishment Church of England. They married two sisters, the daughters of a naval commodore, and lived next door to each other. James had one child, Warwick Oswald; Geoffrey was childless. The brothers died within a year of each other, little more than a decade after the death of their father.

In 1930 Warwick Oswald — at the age of 29 — took charge of the business. Like his grandfather, Warwick was at the helm for 50 years. He had been educated at Geelong Grammar and Oxford. He was tall, gauche and guarded — and interested in philosophy, religion, politics and the arts. Warwick Oswald eventually controlled almost three-quarters of the family shareholding. His cousin Vincent, the son of a younger brother of his father, came to own most of the balance.

During Warwick Oswald's tenure in the family business — from the 1930s to the 1970s — there was a sharp concentration of media ownership in Australia. The key players in this concentration included the Sydney newspaper manager Robert Clyde Packer and his son Frank, and the Melbourne newspaper manager Keith Murdoch and his son Rupert. Media empires grew larger, or they were taken over.

Warwick Oswald took his proprietorship seriously. He also wrote special articles for the *Herald* on subjects of personal interest, such as 'ethics and national life'. But he was not much interested in the details of running a large business. From the 1940s his general manager Rupert Henderson, an intense, driven character, was the driving force behind the business. Henderson defended the *Herald* against its competitors with an intensity that resulted in its dramatic expansion.

Henderson's defensive expansion of John Fairfax and Sons required capital. The privately owned family company was increasingly inadequate as a vehicle for expansion. In 1956 John Fairfax and Sons — after 115 years as a private company — became a public company. The company was still a family business in the sense that family members owned a little more than one-half of the shareholding, but the family control was now more fragile.

In 1959 Warwick Oswald, on Henderson's advice, transferred a large part of his shareholding to his only son, James Oswald. James, named after his grandfather, had also been educated at Geelong Grammar and Oxford. He was already on the company board, alongside his father and his father's cousin Vincent. The reason for the transfer of shares was to avoid death duties. These duties might force successors to sell shares in the company, weakening family

Old families

control. The transfer was designed to ensure a conventional dynastic succession, from father to son.

A conventional dynastic succession did not happen. This was mainly on account of Warwick Oswald's three marriages. In 1945 he left his first marriage, in 1958 he left his second and in 1959 he married a third time. His third wife, Mary, was the daughter of Jewish immigrants from Poland, who had left her own marriage for Warwick Oswald. In 1960 the couple had a son, named Warwick Geoffrey Oswald in the dynastic tradition. Mary Fairfax and the younger Warwick heavily complicated the dynastic succession.

Mary Fairfax became one of Sydney's most lavish society hostesses but struggled for acceptance among the old families of Sydney society. Her husband's first-born son James observed in his memoirs *My Regards to Broadway* that Mary had some success 'where she mainly wanted to succeed' — among the rich, powerful and famous. She was also 'well received by much, but by no means all, of Melbourne society, thanks largely to the exuberant welcomes she ... received from her friend Kath Clarke, whose husband Rupert was one of my father's closest friends in his later years'.

Meanwhile, Sir Warwick — knighted in 1967 — insisted on a more active role in the management of John Fairfax Limited, with the encouragement of his wife. His leadership generated growing tensions among the family and the senior managers. In 1977 the tensions came to a head. Sir Warwick's son James and cousin Sir Vincent, along with the former general manager Rupert Henderson (now 80 years old and a director of the company), demanded that Sir Warwick stand aside in favour of James. Sir Warwick bitterly resigned. One of his friends described him as 'like a wounded tiger'.

Sir Warwick died in January 1987, whereupon the younger Warwick became the bearer of his father's wrath and his mother's ambitions. Warwick had attended Cranbrook and Oxford, and was completing a Master of Business Administration at Harvard. He technically owned almost nothing in John Fairfax Limited, but in the long term he could expect to inherit a big stake in the business. By this time, corporate raiders and media moguls were circling the company like sharks. Warwick believed that the future of the dynasty rested in his hands. He would 'try and take over the company'!

Warwick wanted to prune the family tree, but he didn't really know what he was doing. He recruited self-serving advisors — notably the pugnacious merchant banker Laurie Connell — who gave bad advice for enormous fees. He secured a $2 billion bank loan and privatised the company at the peak of the sharemarket, paying out various corporate raiders (including Robert Holmes à Court), media moguls (including Kerry Packer) and family members. Then in October the sharemarket crashed. The company's profits could not service the interest bill and the privatisation sank under the weight of debt. The tight structure of the family holding had come to an end.

James retired from business and pursued his interests in art and travel. Sir Vincent's son John reinvested the payout to his branch of the family into rural media. Lady Mary beat a path for New York society, but later returned to Sydney. The three different branches of the family still feature in the Rich Lists.

Warwick retreated to Chicago where he lived the life of a recluse. John Lyons, who interviewed him in 1991 for the *Sydney Morning Herald*, reported that he 'stays in his pyjamas for much of the day and rarely leaves the house'. Even so, he seemed relaxed in his new circumstances.

'For the first time in my life,' he told the journalist, 'I'm on my own. I'm a person in my own right rather than the heir to a dynasty.

That's very exciting. Now I rise or fall on my own merits rather than as part of a dynasty.'

The Fairfaxes and the Clarkes are archetypal 'old families'. The brief histories given above are possible precisely because they are old families. The nineteenth century entrepreneurs created businesses and fortunes with legacies reaching out across generations. We know more about these fortunes from the public record than any others on the Rich Lists.

The nineteenth century entrepreneurs were overwhelmingly English and Scottish Protestants. The historian Bill Rubinstein found that these Protestants made up 95 per cent of the people who left behind large fortunes between the 1870s and 1930s. Many of them — like John Fairfax — were devout nonconformists. They exemplified Max Weber's Protestant work ethic.

The first generation struggled to acquire a position in society that matched their wealth. William ('Big') Clarke made more money than anybody, but didn't achieve social standing. The second generation *did* achieve it — becoming prominent in a variety of commercial and social institutions — and did so not only in the colonies but in the 'mother country'. Queen Victoria honoured their achievements: the younger William Clarke became a baronet; James Reading Fairfax became a knight.

Social standing came at the expense of entrepreneurship. From the second generation on, sons were less involved in the businesses through which the first generation accumulated the fortune. Sir James Reading Fairfax, for example, employed a manager on the death of his father. His

> 'WELL, HARKING BACK, THERE IS YOUR FAMILY HISTORY, AS FAR AS I CAN DEPICT IT FOR YOU.'

younger brother Edward retired to England to free himself from the cares of office. Later generations joined the family firm, but professional managers were mainly responsible for running the business.

Also from the second generation on, the handing down of the estate brought a sense of family history and identity. The dynastic names of male children connected them with the past and the future. There are multiple William and Rupert Clarkes. Among the Fairfaxes, there are multiple Johns and Jameses and Warwicks. It is difficult to tell the story of the Clarkes and the Fairfaxes for this reason. It is difficult to distinguish one Sir Rupert from another, or one James Oswald Fairfax from another. Each family is bigger than the individual.

Moreover, sons followed in the footsteps of their forebears. They followed each other to the same schools, notably Geelong Grammar in the first half of the twentieth century. They followed each other to the same universities, notably Oxford. They followed each other in the elite clubs of the colonial capitals. They followed each other in business, in family companies and the directorships of public companies. For example, 'Big' Clarke was a director of the Colonial Bank. His son Sir William was Governor of the Colonial Bank for twenty years. Sir Rupert took his father's place as Governor of the Colonial Bank. When the bank merged to form the National Bank, Sir Rupert's half-brother Sir Frank took his place on the board of directors and served for almost 40 years. The younger Sir Rupert followed his uncle, also serving for almost 40 years.

Over time, the families developed a sense of their own history. In the 1940s, for instance, Sir Frank Clarke wrote a book entitled *The Clarke Clan in Australia* for private distribution. The story began with William Clarke, who made the fortune. Sir Frank then explained that he was only able to trace the descendants of the oldest son William and the youngest son Joseph, who inherited the business fortune between them. He was not able to trace the descendants of Thomas, who had no share in the fortune, and he didn't bother trying to trace the illegitimate children. The flow of money — not genes — shaped the boundaries of the family history.

Sir Frank was a member of the third generation. At the end of his book he passed the baton to the younger generations, and appealed to those still to come. 'Well, harking back,' he wrote, 'there is your family history, as far as I can depict it for you. I ask your pardon for the faults; to keep a true balance was not easy. It is written for the fourth and fifth generations. Let them see to it that there is a sixth and seventh of as good quality. Carry on.'

The younger Sir Rupert Clarke did carry on. His wife Lady Kathleen described the observance of the family history for the benefit of a journalist. In the process she joined together the rough-and-ready 'Big' Clarke and the glittering star of Victorian society, Sir William Clarke, 'Our great grandfather William Clarke came out here from England and worked like a black or a dog, and in 1882 Queen Victoria honoured him by making him a baronet ... We had a wonderful, wonderful party to celebrate 100 years of the Clarke family recently. It was all written up in *Harper's Queens*.'

Not only did one generation of a family come to resemble the one before; old families came to resemble other old families. The men served on the same company boards, belonged to the same clubs, lived in the same suburbs and prayed in the same churches. Their sons attended the same schools and universities. They married one another's sisters and cousins, so that their family trees became intertwined. And it is revealing that the stories of the Clarkes and the Fairfaxes eventually overlapped. Sir Rupert Clarke became the younger Warwick Fairfax's godfather. His wife Lady Kathleen provided an entrée for Lady (Mary) Fairfax in Melbourne society. And from the late 1970s Sir Rupert served as Sir Warwick's alternate director in John Fairfax Limited.

In the 1960s Ernie Campbell's book *The Sixty Rich Families Who Own Australia* conscientiously mapped the interconnections between old families. The Fairfaxes, he observed, were linked through marriage with the Baillieu family. The Baillieus were linked through marriage with the Darling family. The Darlings were linked through marriage with the Clarke family. And so on.

Take the stories of any old families, and there is a good chance of seeing that this type of overlap happens. The overlaps become more textured with each generation, forming the basis of a collective identity and 'society'. In his memoirs James Fairfax observed two definitions of society. The first described it as 'a group of people bound together by a common interest or relationship'. The second defined it as 'the wealthy fashionable social class and their life'.

'Old families bound by ties over several generations,' he wrote, 'like to preserve them through various gatherings, and there is nothing snobbish about this. It simply fulfils the first of the two dictionary definitions.'

Social scientists and commentators were more likely to frame the collective identity and society of old families in terms of 'social class'. Social institutions such as company directorships, clubs, schools and intermarriage forged interconnections between rich families. They became more than a collection of rich families: they became a social class. The density of their interconnections, though, led some commentators to describe them as more than a social class. They were 'the Establishment'.

Sidney Myer, a Jewish immigrant from Russia, assembled a fortune between the 1900s and 1930s. He revolutionised retailing with his Melbourne department store and mass merchandising. At the time old families regarded him as an upstart. They froze him out. In 1919 Myer converted to Christianity. He then wooed and married Merlyn Baillieu, the daughter of an established Melbourne family — linking him by marriage to the Clarkes and the Fairfaxes. He bought a mansion in Toorak, sent his sons to Geelong Grammar, and kept making money. The members of the Melbourne Club never invited him to join their ranks. But they could not ignore him either.

Sidney Myer's will was designed to ensure a Myer dynasty. It provided strong incentives for his two sons, Kenneth and Baillieu, to join the family business. Both sons did so, directing the expansion of the business in the postwar decades. They kept making money. But in 1953 the Melbourne Club rejected Kenneth Myer's nomination as a member, apparently because he was of Jewish descent. In 1970 it also rejected Baillieu's nomination, an act which made national news. Simon Warrender — the second son of an aristocratic English family and a Myer relative by marriage — resigned from the Melbourne Club in protest. Warrender had joined the club in 1950, nominated by Sir Rupert Clarke. In the wake of his resignation from the club he wrote his memoirs, heaping scorn on the Australian 'Establishment' with its 'more-British-than-the-British syndrome'.

At about the same time, Kenneth Myer told the Fairfax-owned *Australian Financial Review* that he did not identify with the Establishment. In his own words: 'Although I am classified as a member of the Establishment, and in a strict sense I am one, certainly in the eyes of the public, I don't classify myself as one because I am a nonconformist.' Kenneth proved his point by opposing Australia's

> 'THE HIGH-FLYERS FLY OVER THEM AND TAKE THE LIMELIGHT, BUT THE ESTABLISHMENT IS STILL THERE.'

involvement in the Vietnam War and advocating the election of Gough Whitlam's Labor Party to government.

The Myer story highlights a contradiction about established wealth. On the one hand, it demonstrates how old families policed their boundaries, closing their ranks against outsiders, with British Protestantism providing a framework of trust. One of my interviewees from an old family makes this point in blunt terms. 'In the Scottish Protestant, capitalist world that I grew up in,' he says, 'there was an unwritten sanction for the very powerful. If somebody misbehaved — the way it was, they were shunned.' Unwritten sanctions kept newcomers like Sidney Myer on the outer. It is revealing that both Kenneth Myer and Simon Warrender spoke of the Establishment in making sense of their experience.

On the other hand, the Myer story also demonstrates the limitations of the Establishment. Old families could not keep newcomers such as Sidney Myer down. The exclusion of his sons from the Melbourne Club was heavily symbolic but ultimately futile. Similarly, established families could not prevent another wave of newcomers in the postwar decades, nor in the tumultuous 1980s when corporate raiders attacked established businesses, including the Fairfax and Myer empires.

The same contradiction informs my interviews with the super rich. On the one hand, some of the people I interview — especially those from old families — dismiss the contemporary relevance of the Establishment. 'It is given a lot more play and a lot more prominence and a lot more longevity than it deserves,' says one man sharply. 'Basically, it has been dead a long time.'

'The Establishment!' another man says ironically. 'It's such a quaint and arcane term. It's great in the popular press, but even there they can't get away with it much any more.'

Old families

On the other hand, some people — especially first-generation entrepreneurs — are emphatic about the enduring influence of established wealth. They have an outsider's perspective. 'They're still there,' says an Adelaide man. 'The highfliers fly over them and take the limelight, but the Establishment is still there.'

'Melbourne is still run by the Melbourne Club in politics and business and wealth,' says an entrepreneur from an immigrant family.

Another Melbourne entrepreneur has no doubt when I ask him whether he has come up against the 'old school tie' network in the course of his business expansion. 'Oh yes, oh yes, yes, very often, yes, oh God yes!' he says.

But even those entrepreneurs who insist most emphatically on the enduring influence of established wealth go on to qualify themselves. The Establishment, they explain, is not entrepreneurial. It is unable to keep the newcomers down. Its institutions — such as Geelong Grammar and the Melbourne Club — are outdated, relics of another era.

Joel Kaplin (an assumed name), for example, is scathing about the Establishment. He runs dismissively through the names of prominent families and then comments on one with a strong pedigree. 'The fact that they lost all their money, because they're stupid fucking idiots and their brains got soggy generation after generation, doesn't matter. They're an established name.' He adds that prominent Jewish businessmen such as Richard Pratt and Solomon Lew will never be accepted by the Establishment. It's a question of breeding,' he explains. 'It's a question of being around at the right time, going to the right school, having the right friends.'

Then again, Kaplin reflects that the Establishment is a shadow of its past. 'Interesting that the Packers aren't Establishment,' he says. 'They've been around for four generations, they're the richest people in Australia, and they're not Establishment. They're entrepreneurial.

'They don't want to be part of the Establishment. They've never played the Establishment game.

'But they're not Establishment, because they don't want to be. They could be, but they don't want to be.'

> 'THE THING IS, FOR A FAMILY THING TO GO ON, EVERYBODY WHO'S IN IT HAS GOT TO WANT TO BE IN IT.'

The handing down of the estate still brings a sense of family history and identity. In the course of interviews I am especially impressed with the Myer family's sense of identity. When I request an interview with a member, I am told that my request will be put before a family subcommittee. I am eventually referred to Stephen Shelmerdine — one of Sidney Myer's grandsons, and the current Chair of the Sidney and Merlyn Myer Family Council.

'My aunt jokes that to be a member of this family is a full-time job,' Shelmerdine says at one point in the interview. 'I tell her, "Well, that used to be true, but now you actually need a secretary and a personal assistant to do all the things — even just to keep in contact."'

Shelmerdine describes a mosaic of family institutions, including several big philanthropic foundations, a family office, the family council, a charter of values, and a 'family muster'. There is a sense in which these institutions and arrangements are the product of Sidney Myer's will — the big philanthropic bequest (one-tenth of his estate) and the various provisions for a dynasty. At the same time, there is more to the mosaic of family arrangements than the dead hand of the past: some of them are innovations of the past decade. They are partly home-grown and partly inspired by overseas example. Above all, they are 'loose structures', designed to make family decision-making processes transparent and accountable — thereby helping to reconcile family continuity and individual ambitions.

The family office, for example, houses the business and philanthropic activities of family members alongside each other. It provides a single location for the family's diverse activities. 'It's primarily organically driven,' Shelmerdine explains, 'though obviously we have had some connections with and influences from other families in Asia, Europe and America.'

The Sidney and Merlyn Myer Family Council includes representatives of all branches, all generations and both the men and women of the family. 'Here the second, third and fourth generation members can meet and discuss things and work on projects which have some influence in the business affairs and some influence in philanthropic affairs. 'But it's more about preserving and enhancing the spirit of the family.'

Every two years the entire extended clan meets for a 'family muster'. 'Everybody goes up into the hills for three days,' Shelmerdine says, 'and we talk about these issues. We have a mixture of fun and reflection and do those corporate problem-solving exercises and brainstorm things, and get to know know one another, and just get a sense of where we can take some projects forward.'

Shelmerdine is acutely aware of the tension between individual autonomy and family continuity. When I ask him about the 'glue' that holds the family together, he stresses that they're 'always trying to ensure that if people want to go off and do their own thing, well, they can'. The family provides a resource for individual members. I ask Shelmerdine how long it can do so, as the family grows larger with each generation.

'Well, it's up to them,' he says. 'It's up to us.'

James Armstrong (as I have called him) — another interviewee from an old family — also describes the evolution of new family institutions and arrangements. The people with fortunes to pass on, he reflects, once thought that there was a much longer period of certainty going into the future. They imagined that they could impose their will over one or two generations through the terms of their wills, resulting in tight institutional structures. 'You'd have to be brave to think that would work now,' Armstrong says. 'The thing is,' he adds, 'for a family thing to go on, everybody who's in it has got to want to be in it. For a family shareholding, it's very difficult.'

Notice here the reference to a 'family thing'. At one time, old families spoke in terms of family tradition and dynasty. Armstrong avoids this type of language, presumably because it sounds pompous and anachronistic. But he is still committed to having a family institutional structure above and beyond the individual. He wants a 'family thing' to go on, and believes that the secret of that lies in having a very loose structure — one which allows family members to maintain a working relationship across generations. It is 'loose' in the sense that it is flexible and voluntary, unlike the family business. It is not difficult to join; it is not difficult to leave. Family members can come and go and can choose their level of involvement.

Armstrong has actively forged such a structure for his own extended family. It rests in a family office, which is just that — a suite of offices at the disposal of family members — but is also much more than that.

'We work together and we pool our resources,' Armstrong explains. Family members share office space, professional services (such as investment managers) and administration (such as secretarial staff). They can also pool their investment capital, enabling them to

Old families

punch above their weight in the market. Or they can take their money out. The flexible arrangement means less stress for family members, and 'has the characteristics to go on for some generations, if that's what people want'.

If that is what people *want*. There's the rub. The old dynastic empires placed family continuity above individual ambitions. This meant that they survived across generations, although it was often at the expense of younger sons and daughters. In a more individualistic age, family institutions give more weight to individual ambitions. Old families become more flexible, more diverse and more open-ended. They are also less likely to survive.

Chapter Eight

The big picture

Secrets of the super rich

> '**I THOUGHT THAT ONE DAY WE MIGHT BECOME SOCIALISTS.**'

The billionaire retailer Gerry Harvey recalls growing up in the 1940s and 1950s. 'You know, when I was a kid,' he reflects, 'I thought that one day we might become socialists, because I thought that the world was heading that way. But I was never a socialist.'

For a large part of the twentieth century, in fact, it seemed that the tide of human history favoured socialism, not capitalism. Early in the century, Communist revolutionaries seized power in Russia and nationalised private property. A little more than a decade later the New York stockmarket — the centre of capitalist enterprise around the world — crashed, bringing on the Great Depression and mass unemployment throughout capitalist societies. Meanwhile, the industrial might of the Soviet Union was going from strength to strength, taking it from a feudal backwater into the league of superpowers. In the wake of World War II, the Soviet Union installed Communist governments across Eastern Europe, while Communists took power in China. Newly independent nation states around the world turned to the Soviet Union and China for leadership and inspiration, turning against their old imperialist rulers from the capitalist world.

During this era, it was socialists and radicals — not business magazines — that compiled 'rich lists'. They did so in order to identify the enemy. They wanted the working class in capitalist societies to get angry about the scale of inequality. They wanted class struggle and social upheaval. For example, Ferdinand Lundberg's *America's 60 Families*, published in 1937, declared that 60 rich families owned and dominated the United States. Lundberg warned that Franklin D. Roosevelt's 'New Deal' — the setting up of a welfare state in the United States — was just a way of fobbing off social unrest in the wake of the Great Depression.

In Australia, as we have seen, Ernie Campbell, a full-time Communist Party organiser, produced his own version of Lundberg's 'rich list' in the early 1960s — *The Sixty Rich Families Who Own Australia*. Campbell was a sometime apprentice tiler who had formed his political beliefs during the Depression. He joined the Communist Party and in 1934 studied Marxist-Leninism at the Lenin School in Moscow. On his return to Sydney he supervised the theoretical education of party recruits. He edited Communist newspapers, including the national *Tribune* in the 1950s, and wrote numerous booklets and pamphlets. By the 1960s he was a member of the Party's Central Committee.

The Sixty Rich Families was Campbell's most ambitious project. According to him, most of the big businesses in Australia at the time were in the hands of these very rich families, who included the Fairfaxes, the Baillieus, the Myers and the Packers. Their monopoly over different sections of the economy meant that they could scoop up huge profits, untroubled by competition. The rich got richer and the poor got poorer.

Ernie Campbell died in a Sydney nursing home in August 1985. Ronald Reagan was President of the United States. Margaret Thatcher was Prime Minister of the United Kingdom. The Soviet Union had embarked upon economic and political liberalisation, which would lead to its unravelling not much later. The world looked very different from the one that Campbell must have anticipated as a young Communist agitator in the 1930s or even in the early 1960s when he wrote *The Sixty Rich Families*.

Campbell's death came in in the same week as the publication of the third edition of the *Business Review Weekly* Rich List. The list was very upbeat. It announced that there was a 'new king of Australia's rich', the Perth entrepreneur Robert Holmes à Court. The magazine observed: 'Like most of those on our rich list — the only empirical study of wealth in Australia — Holmes à Court has made his wealth in his own lifetime.' In an ironic twist, the *BRW* Rich List adopted Ernie Campbell's earlier 'rich list' as a benchmark for comparison. 'Most of the old-money fortunes, nicely documented in E. W. Campbell's [book], have been dissipated,' it noted. 'The wealth spreads among the children and grandchildren, very few of whom manage to build fresh enterprises.'

It was also ironic that the obituary in *Tribune* — where Campbell had once served as editor — celebrated the fact that *Business Review Weekly* had acknowledged the merit of *The Sixty Rich Families Who Own Australia*. There wasn't much else for Communists to celebrate in the 1980s.

Business Review Weekly — owned by the Fairfax family — took the idea of the Rich Lists from *Forbes* magazine in the United States. *Forbes* began its annual survey of the super rich in 1982, *BRW* followed in 1983. At the time, *BRW* was only several years old. It was a new player in a new market, the mass market for business magazines. Robert Gottliebsen was the founding editor — one of a new breed of financial journalists, with a flair for publicity.

When I interview Gottliebsen about the Rich Lists and the super rich, he identifies two reasons for copying the *Forbes* list. The first was competition with the Packer magazine, *Australian Business*. 'The war, which we were not expected to win, was absolutely intense,' Gottliebsen says. 'They were in front.' Each magazine began compiling its own Rich List in order to get a break on the opposition. 'We beat them by about three weeks!' Gottliebsen declares triumphantly.

The second reason for the Rich Lists was ideological. The *BRW* lists — in contrast to the old socialist lists — were a celebration of entrepreneurship, private wealth and capitalism. The super rich were the heroes, not the enemies. Business magazines took up the Rich Lists, Gottliebsen says, because they'd 'woken up to the fact that the game had changed'.

> 'IT'S LIKE THE FIRST PERSON WHO CLIMBS MOUNT EVEREST. THE NEXT CLIMB IS MUCH MORE SKILLED AND A MUCH BETTER JOB. BUT SOMEONE HAD TO DO IT FIRST.'

BRW billed the first Rich List as 'The BRW One Hundred', and organised its entries around the metaphor of a club. There were 'The $100 Million Club', topped by Rupert Murdoch who was valued at $250 million, 'The $50 Million Suite', and 'The Members Pavilion', the last requiring a minimum wealth of $10 million. There was also 'The Family Dress Circle'. Unlike the old elite clubs of the capital cities — the traditional hubs of power, money and prestige in Australia — the Rich List club did did not require an invitation or good breeding. There was one qualification only: money, lots of it.

The inaugural Rich List contained a motley combination of people. Twelve of the family names listed in Campbell's *The Sixty Rich Families* were in it, among them the Fairfaxes, the Myers and the Packers. But the backbone of the list was new money, accumulated by Australian-born and immigrant entrepreneurs since the 1950s and 1960s. As *BRW* observed, there were many names that 'do not appear in *Who's Who*, a very Anglo-Saxon publication, or other reference works of achievement'.

In his editorial introduction, Robert Gottliebsen used the list to tell a very different story from the one told by socialists in earlier times. Most Australians, he wrote, believed 'that big wealth was usually passed down the generations'. The Rich List 'not only explodes the myth, it also shows how we really have a land of opportunity'. He went on: 'Scores of migrants who came to Australia penniless (some swam rivers to escape Eastern Europe) and Australian-born people with relatively small starts have made their fortune under the Southern Cross — and I have no doubt that over the next 20 or 30 years just as many will do it again.'

The Rich List immediately boosted the circulation and profile of *BRW*, giving it an edge over its competition. 'I always say to people that our best Rich List ever was the first one,' Gottliebsen says proudly. 'I'm proudest of our first one.' He pauses. 'You can misinterpret that. Our Rich List now is ten, twenty, thirty times better than the first one, in terms of accuracy and in terms of detail.

'But that first one was the first one, and no one had ever done anything like that before. It's like the first person who climbs Mount Everest. The next climb is much more skilled and a much better job. But someone had to do it first.'

'IT WAS THE SCORE!'

The *BRW* Rich Lists were part of a much larger sea change in capitalist societies, especially the English-speaking countries. In English-speaking countries neo-liberal economic theories — known in Australia as 'economic rationalism' — gained

The big picture

ground, and socialism withered on the vine. In 1983, the year that Australia's inaugural Rich List appeared, Bob Hawke's social democratic Labor Government deregulated the financial system, exposing Australian banks to the gale of foreign competition.

In turn, there was growing turbulence in the world of business. High-profile company raiders attacked giant corporations that had dominated business in preceding decades. The Australian raiders, such as Robert Holmes à Court, Alan Bond and Christopher Skase, assembled business empires and fortunes with astonishing speed, shaking out existing empires in the process. Fuelled by bank credit, the raiders overwhelmingly reorganised assets that had been created by others. This was especially true for Robert Holmes à Court, the biggest raider of them all. In the ABC documentary *Top Floor: the Raider's Tale*, Robert Gottliebsen says of Holmes à Court that he 'saw the making of money as being like a cricket game. "It was the score!" I can remember him saying — and his wife saying — "We can never spend this money. It's impossible to spend it." So it ceased to have any relevance as to personal gain, if you like. It was the score.'

The *BRW* Rich Lists — from 1984, the top 200 fortunes in Australia — celebrated the company raiders as the heroes of the new-style capitalism. The 1986 'Rich 200' drew bold conclusions about the changing character of Australian society:

> A new Australian Establishment is in the making, its fortunes growing with a rapidity not seen since the word 'millionaire' first entered the English language about a century ago. Entrepreneurs are breaking down the boardroom doors, sending 'old' Establishment chairmen off to an illustrious retirement and encouraging salaried managing directors to try their hands at ventures of their own.

Secrets of the super rich

In 1987 the first billionaires appeared on the Rich Lists: Robert Holmes à Court on account of his sharemarket deals, and Kerry Packer on account of selling his television network to Alan Bond for more than a billion dollars. *BRW* gave the occasion a biblical touch, declaring: 'The billionaires cometh.' The new men, it observed, were 'essentially traders, buying other people's assets' — but they were creating 'their own aggregations of substance'. *BRW* went on: 'Look, for instance, at the "substance" of the Bond (private fortune $400 million) and Christopher Skase ($40 million) aggregations after this year's acquisitions. Yet, not so long ago another Establishment saw these two as upstarts.'

Less than six months later the sharemarket crashed. The company raiders had their wealth in the sharemarket and gradually their fortunes unravelled as the banks called in their debts. The raiders resorted to increasingly desperate and sometimes criminal measures to survive, but the 1990 property crash finished most of them off. By 1991 Christopher Skase was on the run and Alan Bond was in court, on his way to prison. Robert Holmes à Court was dead, leaving behind a messy estate for his heirs to sort out. Kerry Packer was the only billionaire left standing.

One *BRW* commentator observed a 'shapelessness' in the surviving big fortunes. The 'new Establishment' was finished before it had begun.

The tide of history had now well and truly turned. In the wake of the Communist collapse in the Soviet Union, the American sociologist Francis Fukuyama described the triumph of markets and liberal democracy as 'the end of history'. In the 1990s, capitalism was the only game left in town. The stockmarket resumed its bull run, fuelled by a wave of new technology.

The big picture

The American economist Paul Krugman observed that the new-technology industries 'brought back what we might call the romance of capitalism: the idea of the heroic entrepreneur who builds a better mousetrap, and in so doing becomes deservedly wealthy'. Since the days of Henry Ford, that heroic figure had come to seem ever more mythical. Giant corporations run by bureaucrats — the 'gray flannel suits' — had increasingly dominated the economy:

> As in the nineteenth century, the economic story became one of remarkable individuals: of men (and, at least occasionally, women) who had a better idea, developed it in their garage or on their kitchen table, and struck it rich. Business magazines actually became interesting to read; and business success came to be seen as admirable, in a way that it hadn't for more than a century.

'THE VERY NATURE OF THE INDUSTRY MEANS YOU EITHER GET BIG OR YOU GET SQUASHED, AND YOU DO IT IN A HURRY, BECAUSE THINGS ARE MOVING QUICKLY.'

The scale of great wealth also became more spectacular than had been the case for more than a century. The most famous figure of the new-technology revolution was the Microsoft founder Bill Gates. In 1996 Gates, at the age of 40, became the richest person in the world. In 1999, at the height of the new-technology boom, the *Forbes* Rich List estimated that he was worth $US85 billion — or about $130 billion in Australian currency. Bill Gates became famous around the world on account of the sheer scale of his wealth. He remains the symbol of the unprecedented riches created in the course of the new-technology revolution at the turn of the millennium.

Economists have struggled to explain the spectacular new fortunes — and runaway economic inequality — appearing in capitalist societies during the 1980s and 1990s. The American economists Robert Frank and Philip Cook, in their book *The Winner-Take-All Society*, suggested that the cause was the spread of 'winner-take-all' markets. Such markets mean that the economy increasingly resembles a kind of tournament in which a few winners get big prizes and most players don't get much at all. It is a bit like the recent crop of high-rating TV shows such as *Big Brother*, *Survivor*, *The Weakest Link*, where the winner walks away with the lot and the losers get nothing.

The classic example of a winner-take-all market has been the entertainment industry, in which a small number of superstars are able to earn phenomenal amounts. Some of these superstars, such as Mel Gibson and Paul Hogan, have featured in the Rich Lists. At the other extreme, the vast majority of performers struggle to make a living, supplementing their earnings by part-time work and welfare.

The reason for the emergence of the modern superstar was that the media increasingly enabled the best entertainers (as judged by the market) to reach huge numbers of people dispersed across space and time. Everyone could see their favourite entertainer on the screen (again and again), rather than a local performer at the neighbourhood hall or a city theatre. In turn, the rewards were concentrated in the hands of a few top performers, with relatively small differences in talent and appeal giving rise to enormous differences in income.

According to Frank and Cook, winner-take-all markets are no longer confined to show business: they now reach across a wide variety of industries and occupations. And in the course of my interviews, entrepreneurs regularly explain the expansion of

The big picture

their business in terms of winner-take-all markets. It is either get big or get out.

One man in a new-economy industry, for example, observes that there's no fifty-year time frame in his business. 'Because of the nature of the industry you're in, you don't have the luxury of spending ten years being small and wondering whether to get big. The very nature of the industry means you either get big or you get squashed, and you do it in a hurry, because things are moving quickly.'

Similarly, Bob Clifford explains how winner-take-all markets forced him to expand his business once he had exhausted the market for passenger boats in Australia. He points out that, whereas it took 40 people to build a passenger boat, it took 200 people to build a much bigger craft able to carry cars and people across Bass Strait. 'But we really didn't have much choice,' he says. 'We either had to stay at a decreasing market share with a work crew of 40, or we had to bite the bullet and go much bigger to a bigger market share.' Clifford bit the bullet but later stumbled when he could not find buyers for a new generation of big boats.

The Rich Lists have reflected the spread of winner-take-all markets. They have charted the rising tide of fortunes among the super rich, including superstars, and kept the score in the winner-take-all society.

'Big money is back,' the 1992 cover spruiked. 'Starring the $178,000-an-hour man, King Kerry, Mel Gibson, INXS, Rose and Gina, Bondy's boys and a full supporting cast.'

'Forty new entrants,' the 2000 edition shouted. 'Three new billionaires. Kerry Packer tops $8 billion.'

'Two new billionaires,' declared the 2001 edition. '15 newcomers. 10 comebacks. Tech fortunes crumble.'

* * *

> **'SOME OF THEM GET THERE BY ALL SORTS OF DEVIOUS MEANS, AND HAVEN'T REALLY BEEN TAUGHT HOW TO EAT WITH A KNIFE AND FORK PROPERLY.'**

In the course of my interviews with the super rich, one entrepreneur — quoted early in this book — expresses his doubts about my research. 'I would be very surprised if you could actually get a common thread through the study that you're undertaking,' he comments. 'I just find that, in my experience, wealth is accumulated in any number of different circumstances.'

When this entrepreneur refers to a common thread, he is partly talking about the big picture and partly about whether I will discover themes across people's stories. But he is talking about more than this. He is questioning whether I will discover shared experiences and interconnections between rich families; for example, in terms of people moving to the same exclusive suburb or joining the same club. More generally, he is questioning whether wealthy people form a collective or group identity. 'I don't strongly identify with other wealthy people,' the entrepreneur explains. 'I've no desire to live in Toorak. I certainly don't seek to gravitate to other people of — shall we say — equal wealth or perceived social stature, or something like that.'

He has a point. In earlier times the common threads were straightforward. Above all, wealthy families were overwhelmingly of English and Scottish Protestant background. In turn, their institutions — such as the Melbourne Club and Geelong Grammar — were grounded in English and Scottish Protestantism. Nowadays, the super rich are multicultural. They include individuals and families of Jewish, Irish Catholic, Greek, Italian, Lebanese and Chinese background. They do not share the same ancestry or religion. They are less likely than was once the case to send their children to the same schools. Their children are less likely to marry each other. They are less likely to feel attached to Great Britain and its aristocratic heritage, including the monarchy.

One immigrant entrepreneur, for example, cannot contain his frustration with the ongoing role of the British monarchy in Australian government. 'I think the Queen is a "parent" to many Australians,' he says. 'They're scared of having their own person stand up in case they don't cut the mustard! I find it very frustrating that in this day and age some bloody woman with a dysfunctional family in England can be the effective Head of State.

'England is just another third-rate country in Europe,' he says dismissively. 'You have to go there to see it!'

Most notoriously, the Establishment clubs exclude some of the super rich from their membership. In the course of my interviews, Jewish and Catholic entrepreneurs regularly comment on their exclusion from such clubs. A man of Catholic upbringing explains why he could not join one of them. 'I wouldn't have the three people to sponsor me,' he says. 'You have to be friends with three people to get in. They would want to be with people of their own kind.'

There is plenty of scope for tensions arising from multiculturalism. Occasionally the tensions register in the interviews. On the one hand, entrepreneurs from non-English-speaking backgrounds are impatient with the Establishment and its exclusive clubs. On the other hand, several interviewees of British ancestry express misgivings about multiculturalism and 'Australian identity'.

One man from old stock, for example, regrets the decline of 'those traditional old families'.

'These other people!' he exclaims. 'Some of them are Johnny-come-latelies. Some of them get there by all sorts of devious means, and haven't really been taught how to eat with a knife and fork properly. So you're eroding values the whole time.'

Later in the interview he returns to the same theme. 'We *were* a Christian country,' he says. 'We're no longer a Christian country. So what are we? We were typified by the good old Aussie digger, who basically came from the western suburbs and the bush. Where are those people now?

'I don't have to tell you what's out in the suburbs now. I mean, it's vastly different.'

But most of the people interviewed — from English-speaking and non-English-speaking backgrounds — overwhelmingly support multiculturalism.

'I think the best thing that has happened to Australia,' says Gerry Harvey, 'is the fact that we're made up of many different cultures and nationalities.'

'That's one of the great things about Australia,' says another man, whose father migrated to Australia. 'You can speak with a thick accent and you can be accepted as a mate. It's great!'

In close connection, interviewees regularly describe established institutions as anachronistic — enclaves of old-fashioned privilege. One man of Protestant upbringing observes that he rarely uses the exclusive club he has joined, 'mainly because the people I meet there are very much the old money'. They are only concerned with 'hierarchical good breeding', good schools and 'correct marriages'.

In turn, the super rich emphasise that trust nowadays arises from individual performance and personal relationships. It depends on what people *do*, not on their family lineage or old school tie. 'I was lucky,' says one man, 'because the industry I worked in was new and evolving. What we did was much more important than the company we kept.'

Similarly, an interviewee from an old family observes that trust is now channelled in a different way from the past. He describes the influence of unwritten sanctions in the Scottish Protestant capitalist world in which he grew up. The unwritten sanctions are much weaker now. 'The level of individual trust is extremely important,' he explains. *'Do I think you are commercial? Do you have what it takes? Or are you one of those bright people who have no idea?* That's very important.

'The trust is not necessarily coming through some sort of wider association. It's much more through individuals.'

Multiculturalism loosened the interconnections between rich families and undercut the Establishment, and in doing so took away one common thread among the super rich. But there are at least three other ways in which the interconnections among wealthy individuals and families have become looser.

'WE ARE MOVING INTO A VERY INDIVIDUALISTIC AGE, I THINK.'

Consider, first, the boards of big public companies governing the commanding heights of the economy. James McNeil (an assumed name), for example, says that his forebears served as directors of big public companies because they usually had a significant stake in the company. In those days the wealth was individual rather than institutional — the owners *were* the owners. Becoming members of the boards of public companies was also 'a way of these people working together'.

Nowadays many of the big public companies are no longer owned by individuals and families. Often they are owned by financial institutions and run by professional managers. The people I interview are rarely interested in serving as directors of these companies.

'I haven't got the time!' says Gerry Harvey. 'I've done those sorts of things in the past. I haven't got the time or the interest.'

Similarly, James McNeil is concentrating on his personal and family investments. He has no interest in public company directorships. 'It's a decision that I made a long time ago,' he says, 'but I think the culture is now going with me. I mean, I think it's an extremely unattractive risk–reward ratio being a director of a public company. You're paid bugger all and you've got extraordinary liabilities.

'You see, really you're representing the Australian institutions: the Australian Superannuation Council and so on. That's not an ambition I have! They can look after themselves.'

Another way in which interconnections among the super rich have become looser relates to political loyalties. For most of the twentieth century, socialists and social democrats challenged the institutions of capitalism. Ernie Campbell's *The Sixty Rich Families Who Own Australia* was a case in point. In turn, class politics caused rich families to get behind the Liberal Party and anti-socialist organisations. For example, Sir Keith Murdoch, Sir Warwick Fairfax and Sir Frank Packer routinely lined their newspapers up behind the Liberals, against the Labor Party.

In the 1980s the tide turned. The *BRW* Rich 200 was a sign of the times. So was the reinvention of the Labor Party under leaders such as Neville Wran, Bob Hawke and Paul Keating. Labor cast off its socialist heritage, forming close links with some of the new entrepreneurs. Equally, there was no longer cause for the super rich to come together against socialism. Commercial competitiveness counted for more; class loyalty counted for less. Bob Hawke told the journalist Paul Barry that Kerry Packer's father was 'a one-party man, a Liberal Party man'. 'One can't say that of Kerry,' he observed. 'He prefers winners to losers.'

The big picture

Most of the people I interviewed still prefer the Liberal Party. They also overwhelmingly subscribe to neo-liberalism, or economic rationalism. Yet they have little interest in politics as a medium of class solidarity. Above all, they are pragmatic in their politics. 'Politicians are in business to be elected and stay in power,' one man explains. 'We're in business to be in business. If you've got a major issue, you've got to try and solve it. Working with government is part and parcel of being in business.'

Some interviewees' disengagement from politics extends further — to lack of interest and to cynicism.

'The whole thing disgusts me!' says one man. 'I haven't voted for twenty years.'

'I don't admire, and I have no passion, one way or another, for government today,' says another man. He ponders for a moment. 'People often ask me,' he continues, '"What is the secret of success?" I say, "Never listen to the news or watch the news, or read the newspaper! If you never do that in your life, you will be successful." And they all laugh. But it's a very serious question.'

A further way in which the interconnections among the super rich have become looser arises from globalisation. In earlier times rich families were interconnected through local and national institutions — such as the Melbourne Club, Geelong Grammar, intermarriage and company directorships. When commentators spoke of an Establishment, they referred to a national network, with regional branches. The strongest regional branches were in Melbourne and Adelaide.

But globalisation means a whole new ball game. The global economy draws many of the super rich overseas. For example, Rupert Murdoch renounced his Australian citizenship in order to develop his media empire in the United States; superstars such as

Mel Gibson and Paul Hogan moved to the United States, the hub of the international entertainment industry; and in the late 1990s cyber entrepreneurs also moved to the United States, the hub of the new economy. Meanwhile, individuals with investment fortunes moved to tax havens in Monaco and the Bahamas.

Even people who reside here are often overseas, pitching their wares. 'The year before last,' says one man, 'I was 140 days away. Last year it was something like 180 days away. This year it's going to be more like 190, 200.' This entrepreneur expects to spend more time overseas in the future because that's where the focus of his business is. 'It's a world market as far as we're concerned,' he explains. 'So we purchase on a worldwide basis and we sell on a worldwide basis. We just happen to manufacture in Australia.

Another self-made entrepreneur — I will call him Mark Jordan — is not sure whether or not his business will remain based in Australia. The Australian market is 'really so small, it's not funny,' he says. 'It's a very good ground for us, because we can test our products. But in the long run, if your major operations are over in Europe, well, you've got to move.'

The 'new' communication technologies, such as video conferencing, mobile phones and email, do not remove the problem of distance. 'You can't do a deal at the video conference,' Jordan explains. 'You can do the nuts and bolts, but you've still got to go and shake their hands. You've got to meet the people, you've got to get the warm and fuzzy feelings. New clients like to *see* you. Bring in a quicker jet and it might be alright!'

It is difficult to find the common threads among the super rich in a global economy. There are still interconnections among rich individuals and families, but the networks are more personal — and more far-flung. The social fabric of the super rich has become a much looser weave than was once the case. And the individual has become more important at the expense of the group — family, class and nation. As one man observes: 'We are moving into a very individualistic age, I think.'

The people I interview only occasionally speak in terms of 'social class'. Mostly they talk about class when they are describing their origins. Bill James, for example, says that the Catholic school he attended had 'a very working-class type background'. Another man talks about his parents' occupations. 'We were from — I would have thought — a lower middle-class background at the time,' he says.

Not one of the interviewees identifies his or her social class in the here and now. Deborah Bryant comes the closest when she describes her difficulty in handling inequalities in her social world. 'Class is a difficult thing,' she remarks. 'Class is a difficult thing.' She goes on to observe that her siblings live in exclusive suburbs, send their children to exclusive schools, and socialise with other people who have inherited fortunes. 'They are actually upper class now,' she says, 'they all mix in totally upper-class circles.'

People are reluctant to talk about their social class in the here and now at least partly because of the taboo surrounding wealth. 'Upper class' evokes associations of superiority and privilege: Bryant, for example, describes the upper class in terms of comfortable complacency. Her siblings, she says, are 'all very comfortable, because they're all in the same boat and they can afford to do the same things'.

> 'YOU LOOK IN THE MIRROR, YOU LOOK AT YOURSELF — WITHOUT ANY BULLSHIT — AND SAY, I'M OKAY.'

More generally, people are reluctant to talk about social class in the here and now because it suggests *inherited* privilege. This is precisely how socialists and radicals in earlier times — such as Ernie Campbell — talked about social class. The idea of class still evokes the image of inherited wealth. And inherited wealth carries a stigma — *more* so than was once the case.

'You're allowed to be rich,' Bryant says, 'if you've made your own money, and that's what everybody aspires to do.'

The people I interview are intensely ambivalent about inherited wealth. On the one hand, they are very largely self-made. Most of them come from modest backgrounds and some come from poverty. Many do not have much of an education. Many experienced trauma and insecurity in the course of their upbringing. They have accumulated amazing new fortunes. They have overshadowed the fortunes of old money.

Entrepreneurs with self-made fortunes take pride in their origins. In close connection, they regularly embody egalitarian values. They are at pains to present themselves as 'ordinary'. In interviews they set an informal tone. They minimise social distance. They use everyday language — including 'fuckin'' this and 'bloody' that. They are overwhelmingly unpretentious.

Recall, for example, the person with whom this book begins. This man is aggressively egalitarian — more so than anyone I interview. He describes how he still does 99 per cent of all his business on a handshake; how he doesn't need to spend money on clothes; how his wife buys bits of cloth at the local market to make dresses for the kids; how he is still 'an old pie-and-sauce man'; how an old docker mate dropped around for a meal the night before; how the family has never had a dishwasher ('the kids have had to wash the dishes').

The big picture

'I think we are a very, very, very basic family — even today,' he comments.

This man is contemptuous of inherited privilege, because inheritance breeds complacency. He says that he loves 'sticking it into the so-called Establishment, or the so-called brainy people. Just to show them, I suppose. Just to show them how stupid they really are. They all go walking around ... but they'll never do the hard yards.'

On the other hand, entrepreneurs with self-made fortunes *have* moved into another world — whether they're willing to admit it or not. They have a galaxy of choices at their feet: they are able to buy homes in the most exclusive suburbs, they are able to send their children to the most exclusive schools, they find themselves invited to join exclusive clubs and become public benefactors, and so on. Hence the lament of Lady Kathleen Clarke: 'Now everybody wants to live in Toorak — everybody who wants to think they're anybody. I mean, it's all changed.'

Above all, the people I interview overwhelmingly plan to leave their money to their children, in one way or another. The children, having been brought up differently, are less constrained by egalitarian values. One woman, for example, describes her parents as inverted snobs. They came from working-class families, made a fortune, but stayed put in the same working-class suburb. 'A fate worse than death for them would be to live in Toorak,' she says. But her privately educated brother and his wife wanted a suburb with 'a lot more status'. They eventually led the second generation's charge to exclusive Toorak.

The man with whom this book begins elaborates on his own ambivalence about inheritance. 'If you don't work for it, you'll never appreciate it,' he explains. 'That is one of the problems of handing down money, handing down wealth to families, and things like that.

Secrets of the super rich

You've got to be very, very careful, because the ones who come along later on have never done the hard yards.

'And because they've got the money,' he goes on, 'what do you reckon they'll be then? They'll be fuckin' educated, because they want to live up to an image, d'you know what I mean.

'But it's natural that you want the best for your children ...'

The secret of making a new fortune is doing the hard yards, along with single-minded opportunism and getting into the right line of business. The secret of what to do with the fortune is more elusive. Hence the fears of the man above about his children's education. Hence too the complicated trust arrangements of Bill Pease; the anguished decision of Gerald Singer to give his money away; the torturous suicide of Brendan Moran; the 'secret life' of Deborah Bryant; and the myriad family secrets among the super rich.

Gerald Singer's account of giving away his money is especially revealing. 'I say to myself, "The more that I give, the happier I feel about myself and the more I can look at myself in the mirror and say, you're okay."'

I think that Singer is not only describing the impulse that makes him give his money away: he is also describing what drove him to make the money in the first place.

'You look in the mirror, you look at yourself — without any bullshit — and say, *I'm okay.*'

References

ABC television documentary, *Top Floor: The Raider's Tale*, ABC, 6 August 1998

Barry, P., *The Rise and Rise of Kerry Packer*, Bantam, Sydney, 1993, p. 244

Blitz, R. and Siegfried, J., 'How Did the Wealthiest Americans Get So Rich?', *The Quarterly Review of Economics and Finance*, 32(1), 1992

Business Review Weekly Rich List quotations from the 1980s can be found in the following editions: 16 August 1985, p. 69; 12–18 November 1983, p. 23; 15 August 1986, p. 47; 14 August 1987, p. 42; 12 May 1989, p. 52; and discussing the Clarkes, 20 December 1985, p. 38

Cadzow, J., 'Last of the True Blue Bloods,' in *The Good Weekend* (magazine within the *Sydney Morning Herald* and *The Age*), 17 November 1990, pp. 10, 18

Cadzow, J., Agenda, *Sunday Age*, 18 February 1996, p. 6

Campbell, E.W., *The Sixty Rich Families Who Own Australia*, Current Books, Sydney, 1963

Cannon, M., *Life in the Cities*, 2nd edn, Viking O'Neil, Ringwood, 1988, p. 164

Clarke, F., *The Clarke Clan in Australia* (privately printed), Baillieu Library, 1946, p. 45

Clarke, M., *'Big' Clarke*, Queensberry Hill Press, Melbourne, 1980

Clarke, M., *Clarke of Rupertswood 1831–1897: The Life and Times of William John Clarke First Baronet of Rupertswood*, Australian Scholarly Publishing, Melbourne, 1995

Collins, J., Gibson, K., Alcorso, C., Castles, S. and Tait, D., *A Shop Full of Dreams: Ethnic Small Business in Australia*, Pluto, Sydney, 1995

Dunstan, K., 'The Clarkes: Grandpa Owned a Regiment,' in *The Bulletin*, 20 February 1979, pp. 58–9

Edgar, P., *Janet Holmes à Court*, HarperCollins, Sydney, 1999, p. 5

Fairfax, J., *My Regards to Broadway: A Memoir*, Angus & Robertson, Sydney, 1991, pp. 101, 294–5, 299, 307

Flannery, T., *The Future Eaters: An Ecological History of the Australasian Lands and People*, Reed New Holland, Sydney, 1994, pp. 284–8

Fukuyama, F., *Trust: The Social Virtues and the Creation of Prosperity*, Penguin, London, p. 21

James, B., *Top Deck Daze: Adventures on the Frog and Toad*, Halbrooks Publishing, Avalon, 1999, pp.10–17

Kiddle, M., *Men of Yesterday: A Social History of the Western District of Victoria 1834–1890*, Melbourne University Press, Melbourne, 1961

Krugman, P., *The Return of Depression Economics*, Allen Lane, London, 1999, p.15

Frank, R. and Cook, P., *The Winner-Take-All Society: Why the Few at the Top Get So Much More Than the Rest of Us*, Penguin, New York, 1996

Landes, D., *The Wealth and Poverty of Nations: Why Some Are So Rich and Some Are So Poor*, Norton, New York, 1999, pp 174–9, 516

Lyons, J., 'Once there was a dynasty,' in *The Good Weekend* (magazine within the *Sydney Morning Herald* and *The Age*), 2 November 1991, pp. 25–6

Mant, A., *Intelligent Leadership*, Allen & Unwin, Sydney, 1997

Marceau, J., *Small Manufacturing Enterprises in Australia: Owners, Operations and Employment Policies: Report on a Pilot Study in Sydney and Melbourne*, Ministry of Employment and Training, Melbourne, 1983

Margo, J., *Frank Lowy: Pushing the Limits*, HarperCollins, Sydney, 2000, pp 26–7, 55, 66, 89, 185–6, 288

Martin, J. and Meade, P., *The Educational Experience of Sydney High School Students: Report No. 1*, AGPS, Canberra, 1979

McLaren, S., 'The Relationship between the Perceived Control of Stressful Life Events, Thought Suppression and the Symptoms of Obsessive-compulsive Disorder,' DPsych thesis, La Trobe University, 2000

McIntyre, S., *The Reds: The Communist Party of Australia from Origins to Illegality*, Allen & Unwin, Sydney, 1999

Myer, R., *Living the Dream: The Story of Victor Smorgon*, New Holland, Sydney, 2000, pp. 285–7

Obituary of Ernie Campbell, *Tribune*, 4 September 1985

Ostrow, R., *The New Boy Network: Taking Over Corporate Australia*, William Heinemann, Richmond, 1987, pp. 59, 276

Playford, J., 'Myth of the Sixty Families', *Arena*, no. 23, 1970

Power, P., *From These Descended*, Homestead Books, Kilmore, 1977, pp. 167, 174, 178–9

Rubinstein, W. D., 'Wealth in Australia', *Quadrant*, June 1980

Salter, R., 'Flinders Lane ... Memory Lane', Jewish Historical Society, 1989, 10(7), pp. 583–89

Sarachek, B., 'American Entrepreneurs and the Horatio Alger Myth', *Journal of Economic History*, 38(2), University of Pennsylvania, 1978

Siegfried, J., Blitz, R. and Round, D., 'The Limited Role of Market Power in Generating Great Fortunes in Great Britain, the United States and Australia', *The Journal of Industrial Economics*, 43, Blackwell, England, 1995

Siegfried, J. and Roberts, A., 'How Did the Wealthiest Britons Get So Rich?', *Review of Industrial Organization*, 6(1), De Kluwer Academic Publishers, The Netherlands, 1991

Souter, G., *Company of Heralds*, University of Melbourne Press,1981

Sowell, T., *Race and Culture: A World View*, BasicBooks, New York, 1994

Stanley, T. J. and Danko, W. D., *The Millionaire Next Door: The Surprising Secrets of America's Wealthy*, HarperBusiness, Sydney, 1996

Sykes, T., *Operation Dynasty*, Greenhouse, Melbourne, 1989

Waldren, M., *Moran v. Moran*, HarperCollins, Sydney, 2001

Warrender, S., *Score of Years*, Wren, Melbourne, 1973, p. 136

Wilson, V., *The Secret Life of Money: Exposing the Private Parts of Personal Money*, Allen & Unwin, Sydney, 1999, pp. 36, 53, 161

Williamson, K., 'Children of the Rich: Living with a Sense of Entitlement,' in *The National Times*, 25–31 March 1983, p. 9

About the author

Dr Michael Gilding is Associate Professor in Sociology and Director of the Centre for New Technologies and Society at Swinburne University of Technology in Melbourne.

He has written extensively on the family, family businesses, and entrepreneurship, including two books and numerous articles.

Michael Gilding is currently working on a companion book to *Secrets of the Super Rich* about the new wave of high-technology entrepreneurs.

www.ingramcontent.com/pod-product-compliance
Lightning Source LLC
Chambersburg PA
CBHW022013290426
44109CB00015B/1156